B.J. Summers' POCKET GUIDE TO Coca-Cola®

Identifications
Current Values
Circa Dates

COLLECTOR BOOKS
A Division of Schroeder Publishing Co., Inc.

The current values in this book should be used only as a guide. They are not intended to set prices, which vary from one section of the country to another. Auction prices as well as dealer prices vary greatly and are affected by condition as well as demand. Neither the Author nor the Publisher assumes responsibility for any losses that might be incurred as a result of consulting this guide.

On the Cover:

Clockwise from top:

Ty Cobb, sports favorite, one of set of ten, $110.00
1941 skater tray, $325.00
Silhouette Girl, thermometer, $375.00
Aluminum six pack carrier, 1950, $75.00
1950s Taiyo van, $225.00
Amber script bottle, $55.00
Salesman sample, box cooler, $900.00

Cover design by Beth Summers
Book design by Karen Smith

Additional copies of this book may be ordered from:

Collector Books
P.O. Box 3009
Paducah, Kentucky 42002-3009

@$9.95. Add $2.00 for postage and handling.

Contents

Paper, window display, see page 33 for listing.

Acknowledgments

I would like to extend my sincere thanks to the following people and businesses without whose help this book would have been impossible.

Alfred and Earlene Mitchell
c/o Collector Books
P.O. Box 3009
Paducah, KY 42002-3009

One of the nicest couples you could ever know, who have been collecting since the sixties. They were kind enough to allow us to photograph much of their collection and answer a constant stream of questions. Al and Earlene are very active collectors. They buy, sell, trade, and are very active in collectors' clubs.

Riverside Antique Mall
P.O. Box 4425
Sevierville, TN 37864
Ph. 423-429-0100

Located in a new building overlooking the river, this is a collector's heaven. It's full of advertising, with lighted showcases and plenty of friendly help. You need to allow at least half a day for a quick look through this place that sits in the shadows of the Smokey Mountains.

Affordable Antiques Inc.
933 S. 3rd St.
Paducah, KY 42001
Ph. 502-442-1225

Easy to find on Paducah's I–24 loop, Oliver Johnson usually has some Coke collectibles worth the visit. If you don't find what you need, he can usually locate it for you.

Gary Metz's Muddy River Trading Co.
263 Lakewood Dr.
Moneta, VA 24121
Ph. 540-721-2091, Fax 540-721-1782

If you are a collector of Coca-Cola, you need to know about The Muddy River Trading Co. Gary has a couple of great auctions each year that offer us a chance at both very rare and common collectibles. He also has a good supply of advertising in stock. And all of his merchandise is guaranteed. I've always found him to be extremely helpful and totally honest. I recommend him highly. See ad in back of book!

Collector's Auction Service
Rt. 2 Box 431, Oakwood Dr.
Oil City, PA 16301
Ph. 814-677-6070

Mark Anderton and Sherry Mullen offer a couple of great mail and phone advertising auctions each year. While their main focus is on oil and gas collectibles, there have been a good many Coca-Cola collectibles offered. It is worthwhile to check them out.

Creatures of Habit
406 Broadway
Paducah, KY 42001
Ph. 502-442-2923

This business will take you back in time with its wonderful array of vintage clothing and advertising. If you are ever in western Kentucky, stop and see Natalya and Jack.

Acknowledgments

The Illinois Antique Center
308 S.W. Commercial
Peoria, IL 61602
Ph. 309-673-3354

Situated on the river in downtown Peoria, this remodeled warehouse is full of great advertising. You need to plan on spending the day here. There's always plenty of courteous help for your convenience.

Chief Paduke Antiques Mall
300 S. 3rd St.
Paducah, KY 42003
Ph. 502-442-6799

This full-to-overflowing mall is located in an old railroad depot in downtown Paducah with plenty of general line advertising, including good Coke pieces, plus a good selection of furniture. Stop by and see Charley or Carolyn if you're in this area.

Pleasant Hill Antique Mall
& Tea Room
315 South Pleasant Hill Rd.
East Peoria, IL 61611
Ph. 309-694-4040

One day won't be enough time to look through this stuffed-full warehouse mall. Bob Johnson has a great place for collectors. You can shop until you're ready to drop then have a great meal at the tea room conveniently located in the center of the mall. It has plenty of friendly help and multiple cashier stations.

Antiques, Cards, and Collectibles
203 Broadway
Paducah, Ky 42001
Ph. 502-443-9797

Three floors of antiques and collectibles housed in an old historic hardware store in downtown Paducah. Owner Ray Pelley offers a good array of collectibles along with some great Coca-Cola collectibles.

Michael and Debbie Summers
3258 Harrison St.
Paducah, KY 42001

My sincere thanks to my brother and sister-in-law for all their help tracking down collectibles and collectors.

Poster, cardboard, cut out, "Season's Greetings," see page 131 for listing.

If I have omitted anyone who should be here, please be assured it is an oversight on my part and was not intentional.

Pricing

The intent of this book is to help familiarize the collector with current market values. It is not designed to influence or help set those values. There are several factors that affect values, and condition and location are probably the two biggest.

Condition should be a prime factor in determining value. If you are buying a collectible that is in good condition, the price shouldn't be the same as a mint piece. Unfortunately we all see mint prices being placed on fair and good collectibles almost daily. The prices given in this book reflect the condition of the specific item as stated in each listing.

1936, 50th Anniversary, see page 58 for listing.

Location will also play a part in determining value. In the Midwest where I live, values will generally be less that in the Northeast or on either coast. However remember there are always exceptions to every rule.

Rarity will also play a part in the value of a collectible. How often will you see the piece? And how badly do you want it? Will you see it later on down the road at a better price? All of these questions play a part in determining value.

In addition to this book there are several good reference sources on the market to help with buying and pricing. *Schroeder's Antiques Price Guide*, *Goldstein's Coca-Cola Collectibles*, B.J. Summers' *Value Guide To Advertising Memorabilia*, and *Huxford's Collectible Advertising*, all available from Collector Books, are excellent reference sources.

Wood, Sprite Boy Welcome Friend, see page 53 for listing.

No other single product has captured the heart of the American public like Coca-Cola. We all have memories that relate to this magic elixir. It might be a high school ball game with popcorn and Coke, or a date at the local drive-in sharing a cherry Coke. Ever since the days of Dr. J.S. Pemberton and Asa Griggs Chandler, Coca-Cola has provided us with America's favorite soft drink. And even though it has been with us over a century, its closely guarded formula has changed little. That is an unusual accomplishment especially for a product that has affected our entire culture.

The Coca-Cola Company has helped launch the career of many fine artists. And has made the work of several accomplished artists familiar in households across the country. Although Norman Rockwell may be best known for his work as a cover illustrator for *Saturday Evening Post*, he also did art work for Coca-Cola. Two prominent examples are the calendars for 1931 and 1932. And who can think of Christmas without the Coca-Cola Santa Claus coming to mind. The artist Haddon Sundblom created the most popular version of the Coca-Cola Santa Claus.

Over the years many soft drinks have come and gone. But Coca-Cola remains a leader due primarily to the proliferation of wonderful advertising and the company's ability to generate a great product.

I hope this book in some way will broaden your collecting experience and help acquaint you with the values of those collectibles.

Autumn Leaves, five piece festoon, designed for use on a soda fountain back bar, 1927, G, $900.00.

Bottle topper, Canadian, great graphics by Fred Mizen, "Refresh Yourself," 1926, 13" x 13", EX, $3,600.00.

Canvas awning, Refreshment Center, red & white stripe, 1950s, 5' x 2', EX, $575.00.

Photos courtesy Muddy River Trading Co./Gary Metz

Signs

Bottle hanger, Santa Claus in refrigerator full of bottles, being surprised by small child, 1950s, M $5.00

Bottle topper, plastic, "We let you see the bottle," 1950s, EX....$400.00

Canvas banner, "Take Coke Home," pricing information at bottom, 24 bottle case in center, 9' tall, EX ..$150.00

Cardboard, bather in diamond blue background pictured with a Coke button and a bottle, framed and under glass, 1940, 23" x 22", NM $1,400.00

Cardboard, bather in round blue background, framed and under glass, by Snyder & Black, rare, 1938, 22", NM $2,000.00

Cardboard, Canadian poster featuring artwork of girl on ping pong table with a bottle of Coke, framed under glass, 14" x 28", G......$600.00

Cardboard, Canadian trolley card, "Drink Coca-Cola, Made In Canada," 1920s, 21" x 11", F $170.00

Cardboard, carton insert, "Good With Food," 1930s, NM $150.00

Cardboard, cut out, Coca-Cola policeman, waist up view with "Stop for pause, Go refreshed" ribbon in front, great graphics, hard to find, 1937, 45" x 32", G, $1,050.00.

Cardboard, cut out, woman with glass of Coke, similar to 1930 serving tray, 1930, 21" x 38", F, $525.00.

Cardboard, die cut, fishing boy and dog with original pond, unusual find, 1935, 36" tall, G, $2,500.00.

Photos courtesy Muddy River Trading Co./Gary Metz

Cardboard clown balancing on a bottle, 1950, EX $800.00

Cardboard, Coca-Cola polar bear stand up , 6' tall, EX $65.00

Cardboard, cut out, "Buy Coca-Cola, Have for Picnic Fun," shows two couples having a picnic, 1950s, EX....................................... $95.00

Cardboard cut out, "Drink Coca-Cola, The Pause that Refreshes," used as a window display by Niagara Litho Co. N.Y, 1940s, 32½" x 42½", G $800.00

Cardboard, cut out, featuring glass in hand, has a 3-D effect, 1958, 19" x 21", G $300.00

Cardboard, cut out, model with a bottle and a colorful parasol, easel back, 1930s, 10" x 18½", EX $1,500.00

Cardboard, cut out, orchid festoon component, 1939, 30" x 18", G..$200.00

Cardboard, cut out, sign with elves and a bottle on sled, 12" x 20", EX ..$180.00

Cardboard, die cut, festoon centerpiece featuring soda jerk, scarce, 1931, G................................$1,600.00

Cardboard, dimensional arrow sign, heavy brown cardboard, hard to find, 1944, 20" x 12", G, $150.00.

Cardboard, die cut, sailor girl with "Take Home" flags, matted and framed, 1952, 11" x 7", NM, $375.00.

Cardboard, double sided, Canadian, horizontal poster, featuring woman serving Coca-Cola on one side and a bottle in snow bank on reverse, 1950s, 36" x 20", G, $180.00.

Photos courtesy Muddy River Trading Co./Gary Metz

Cardboard, die cut, French Canadian string hanger with great graphics featuring woman with a Coke, 1939, 15" x 22", G........................$1,600.00

Cardboard, die-cut sailor girl, 1952, 11" x 7", NM $350.00

Cardboard, die cut, string hanger featuring Sprite Boy with bottle cap hat, "Drink Coca-Cola, Be Refreshed," Canadian, 1950s, 11" wide, NM $2,200.00

Cardboard, die cut, "Take Enough Home," bottle in hand, 1952, VG $160.00

Cardboard die cut with attached hangers for wall or window display, Bathing Girl, 1910, F........$1,450.00

Cardboard, double sided, Canadian poster featuring woman with bottle on both sides, different backgrounds, 1950s, 56" x 27", G $220.00

Cardboard, "Drink Coca-Cola Delicious and Refreshing" sign with tin frame featuring 1915 bottle on each side, 1910s, 60" x 21", NM ..$1,450.00

Cardboard, easel back French Canadian sign "Coke Convient," 1948, 18" x 24", NM $200.00

Cardboard, embossed die cut easel back sign featuring girl in woods illustrated in a beveled mirror with advertising at bottom marked "Kaufmann and Strauss Company, New York," 1903, 4½" x 10½", EX, $15,500.00.

Cardboard, easel back Kit Carson promotional sign, promoting kerchief, 1950s, 16" x 24", EX, $200.00.

Cardboard, "Have a Coke" sign featuring Sprite Boy advertising King Size, has a hanger and easel back attachment, 1957, 18" sq, EX, $170.00.

Photos courtesy Muddy River Trading Co./Gary Metz

Cardboard, easel back or hanging sign featuring a glass of Coke, Canadian, 1949, 12' x 12", EX $120.00

Cardboard, easel back sign "thirst asks nothing more" featuring bottle in hand, 1939, 12" x 16", NM $1,800.00

Cardboard, festoon elements featuring man and woman with magnolias, great graphics, 1938, G........$600.00

Cardboard, festoon unit "Shop Refreshed" featuring couple with a glass of Coke, 1950s, 29" x 14", EX $210.00

Cardboard, French Canadian poster, woman shopper, 1950s, EX ..$150.00

Cardboard, French Canadian sign featuring bottle in snow bank, 1950s, 22" x 50", EX $150.00

Cardboard, French Canadian, girl in front of box cooler with bottle in hand, original easel back stand, 1940s, 12" x 17", EX $225.00

Cardboard, horizontal, "Accepted Home Refreshment," couple with popcorn and Coca-Cola in front of fireplace, "Drink..." button lower right, 1942, 56" x 27", G $175.00

Cardboard, horizontal featuring silhouette girl running, "Let's watch for 'em," 1950s, 66" x 32", NM, $800.00.

Cardboard, horizontal poster "Coke time" featuring three women at table, 1943, EX, $475.00.

Cardboard, horizontal poster "Coke... For Hospitality" featuring artwork of people at cook out, framed under glass, 1948, 36" x 24", NM, $425.00.

Photos courtesy Muddy River Trading Co./Gary Metz

Cardboard, horizontal, "Be Really Refreshed," scene of couple in boat on pond, 1960s, 36" x 20", EX $85.00

Cardboard, horizontal, "Drink Royal Palm Beverages Made from Pure Cane Sugar by the Coca-Cola Bottling Company," 1930s, 17" x 11¼", F......................$60.00

Cardboard, horizontal "Have a Coke," young cheerleader with megaphone and a bottle, "Coca-Cola" button on right, 1946, 36" x 20", G.................................$225.00

Cardboard, horizontal, "Here's Something Good!", woman with crown, man in clown suit with bottle, 1950s, 56" x 27", G $200.00

Cardboard, horizontal, "Inviting you to refreshment," EX ..$650.00

Cardboard, horizontal poster "Coke is Coca-Cola" in original gold frame, 1949, EX $500.00

Cardboard, horizontal poster featuring artwork of woman at microphone with a bottle of Coke "Entertain your thirst," 1941, 36" x 20", EX $500.00

Cardboard, horizontal poster featuring Sprite Boy advertising family size too, in original wooden frame, 1955, 36" x 20", EX, $500.00.

Cardboard, horizontal poster featuring Sprite Boy with six pack of Coke, 1946, 41½" x 27½", F, $525.00.

Cardboard, horizontal poster, "You taste its quality" featuring artwork of woman with flowers and a bottle of Coke, framed under glass, 1942, 36" x 20", NM, $1,150.00.

Photos courtesy Muddy River Trading Co./Gary Metz

Cardboard, horizontal poster featuring bottle in ice "Have a Coke," 1944, 36" x 20", NM $300.00

Cardboard, horizontal poster featuring Coke crossing guard, "Let's watch for 'em," 1950s, 66" x 32", NM $800.00

Cardboard, horizontal poster, featuring a lunch counter scene, "A great drink with food," Canadian, 1942, 36" x 20", G $525.00

Cardboard, horizontal poster featuring people in a picnic scene with a cooler, 1954, 36" x 24", EX ..$400.00

Cardboard, horizontal poster "How about a Coke" featuring artwork of three girls at counter, 1939, G..$450.00

Cardboard, horizontal poster in original Kay Displays frame featuring two couples by fire, 1954, 36" x 24", G $400.00

Cardboard, horizontal poster, "Play Refreshed" girl in cowboy hat, 1951, EX $325.00

Cardboard, horizontal poster with circus scene "Here's Something Good" in original repainted frame without applied detail, 1951, EX $350.00

Cardboard, large horizontal "Mind Reader," woman on chaise being offered a bottle of Coke, EX, $625.00.

Cardboard, large horizontal poster, double sided with a young couple on one side and a fishing girl on the other, 1950s, F, $230.00.

Cardboard, large horizontal poster featuring park scene with Coke iced down in a tub, hard to find item, 1952, F, $300.00.

Photos courtesy Muddy River Trading Co./Gary Metz

Cardboard, horizontal, "Refreshing," woman in white dress at counter with a bottle, 1949, 56" x 27", VG $375.00

Cardboard, horizontal sign featuring girl with bottle and menu, 1960s, 66" x 32", NM $650.00

Cardboard, "I'm heading for Coca-Cola," woman in uniform getting off airplane, in original wood frame, 1942, 16" x 27", VG..............$600.00

Cardboard, Italian horizontal poster with a woman and a Coke bottle, 1940s, 36" x 20", NM $425.00

Cardboard, "it's Twice Time, Twice the value," 1960s, 66" x 32", NM ..$800.00

Cardboard, large horizontal poster featuring hot dog roast, "Coca-Cola belongs," 1942, EX $400.00

Cardboard, large horizontal poster, cowgirl with bottle, 1951, G..$375.00

Cardboard, large horizontal poster featuring sailor girl in original frame, 1940, F $400.00

Cardboard, large horizontal truck side poster featuring mod couple on a motor scooter, 1960s, 67" x 32", NM..$210.00

Cardboard, lobby poster featuring Clark Gable and Joan Crawford, Dancing Lady, 1930s, EX, $1,900.00.

Cardboard, large vertical poster "Mom knows her groceries," featuring woman at refrigerator, 1946, G, $400.00.

Cardboard, panoramic view poster of couple in front of touring car, 1924, 32½" x 18", EX, $800.00.

Photos courtesy Muddy River Trading Co./Gary Metz

Cardboard, large vertical poster featuring girl on diving board, 1939, G $450.00

Cardboard, large vertical poster featuring girl with horse, 1938, EX ..$1,000.00

Cardboard, large vertical poster featuring ice skater, 1940s, F......$80.00

Cardboard, "New Family Size too!", Sprite Boy advertising Coca-Cola all on yellow background, 1955, 16" x 27", NM $155.00

Cardboard oval, string hung, denoting price, German, 1930s, EX..$95.00

Cardboard, "Party Pause," woman in clown suit, 1940s, 36" x 20", G..$350.00

Cardboard, "Pause," clown and an ice skater, in original wooden frame, 1930s, EX.............$800.00.

Cardboard, poster, "At Ease... for refreshment," military nurse in uniform holding a bottle, in original wooden frame, 1942, NM $1,000.00

Cardboard, poster, "The best is always the better buy," girl with grocery sack and six pack, framed under glass, 1943, EX..........$975.00

Cardboard, poster featuring Sprite Boy displaying two bottle sizes, 1955, 16" x 27", NM, $250.00.

Cardboard, poster featuring Hostess Girl, artwork by Hayden, 1935, 29" x 50", G, $2,100.00.

Cardboard, poster featuring three women "Friendly Pause," 1948, 16" x 27", NM, $1,500.00.

Photos courtesy Muddy River Trading Co./Gary Metz

Cardboard, poster, "Big Refreshment," girl with bowling ball, 1960s, 66" x 32", NM $650.00

Cardboard, poster, "Coke Time," cover girl with original frame, 1950s, 16" x 27", NM $750.00

Cardboard, poster, double sided, "Have A Coke" and Skater Girl on one side with "Refresh Yourself" with horses and riders, 1955, 16" x 27", VG $200.00

Cardboard, poster, "Easy To Take Home," 1941, EX $350.00

Cardboard, poster featuring ballerinas, "entertain your thirst," 1942, 16" x 27", F $125.00

Cardboard, poster featuring cartoon spaceman, 1960s, NM....................$160.00

Cardboard, poster featuring cheerleader "Refresh yourself," 1944, 16" x 27", NM $1,150.00

Cardboard, poster featuring elves with a carton on wagon, "Take enough Home," 1953, 16" x 27", G $170.00

Cardboard, poster featuring girl at refrigerator, 1940, 16" x 27", EX..$700.00

Muddy River Trading Co./Gary Metz

Cardboard, poster, "Good taste for all," 1955, 16" x 27", NM, $225.00.

Muddy River Trading Co./Gary Metz

Cardboard poster, horizontal, "All set at our house," with boy holding cardboard six pack carrier, 1943, EX, $650.00.

Cardboard, poster, horizontal, "Face your job refreshed," woman wearing visor beside a drill press, 59" x 30", VG, $600.00.

Cardboard, poster, girl against a rock wall, resting from bicycle riding, from Niagara Litho, 1939, VG........$375.00

Cardboard, poster, "Have A Coke," a bottle against an iceberg, 1944, 36" x 20",G.................................$275.00

Cardboard, poster, horizontal, "Coke for me, too," couple with bottles and a hot dog, 1946, 36" x 20", EX....$185.00

Cardboard, poster, horizontal, "The drink they all expect," couple getting ready to entertain with finger sandwiches and iced bottles, 1942, NM $600.00

Cardboard, poster, horizontal, "Got enough Coke on ice?" three girls on sofa, one with phone receiver, framed, Canadian, 1945, G...................$250.00

Cardboard, poster, horizontal, "Here's to our G.I. Joes," 1944, VG $750.00

Cardboard, poster, horizontal, "Hospitality Coca-Cola," girl lighting a candle with a bottle in foreground, 1950, 59" x 30", VG..............$700.00

Cardboard, poster, horizontal, "Hospitality in your hands," woman serving four bottles from tray, 1948, 36" x 20", EX $250.00

Cardboard poster, horizontal, "Thirst knows no season," woman drinking from a bottle in front of skiers, framed, 1940, 56" x 27", EX, $450.00.

Muddy River Trading Co./Gary Metz

Cardboard, poster in frame, featuring girl in swim suit with a bottle of Coke, "Yes," 1947, 15" x 25", F, $375.00.

Cardboard, poster, horizontal, "What I want is a Coke," girl on sandy beach in swim suit reaching for a bottle, in original wooden frame, hard to find, 1952, E, $1,100.00.

Cardboard, poster, horizontal, "Lunch Refreshed," 1943, EX............$1,000.00

Cardboard, poster, horizontal, majorette, "Refresh," 1952, 36" x 20", VG $475.00

Cardboard, poster, horizontal, "Now! for Coke," trapeze artist reaching for bottle, framed, 1959, 27" x 21", VG.......................$300.00

Cardboard, poster, horizontal, "The pause that refreshes," girl on a chaise holding a bottle, 1942, 36" x 20", VG $95.00

Cardboard, poster, horizontal, "Play refreshed," woman in cap with fishing rig and a bottle, 1950s, 36" x 20", VG $300.00

Cardboard, poster, horizontal, "The rest-pause that refreshes," three women in uniform, 1943, 36" x 20", EX $425.00

Cardboard, poster, horizontal, "Why grow thirsty," 1945, 36" x 20", VG.......................................$150.00

Cardboard, poster, horizontal, "Zing together with Coke," party scene, cooler on table, 1962, 37" x 21", G..$200.00

Cardboard poster, large horizontal, "Good Pause Drink Coca-Cola in Bottles," 1954, 36" x 20", G, $500.00.

Cardboard poster, vertical, "The drink they all expect," similar to horizontal poster of this year but showing full length art work of couple preparing for entertaining, 1942, EX, $700.00.

Cardboard poster, vertical, "Coke Time," in original wooden frame, 1943, EX, $950.00.

Cardboard, poster, large horizontal, "a Coke belongs," young boy and girl with a bottle, in original Coke frame, 1944, EX......$950.00

Cardboard, poster of woman with straw hat in water , 1960s, 36" x 20", EX $75.00

Cardboard, poster, one part of a series, "Through the years" with Victorian era advertising, 1939, 16" x 27", NM $950.00

Cardboard, poster "Things go better with Coke" in original frame, 1960s, 16" x 27", F $250.00

Cardboard poster, vertical, "Extra-Bright Refreshment," couple at party holding bottles, 33" x 53", G......$200.00

Cardboard, poster, vertical, "Face the sun refreshed," pretty girl in white dress shielding her eyes from the sun with one hand while holding a bottle with the other, 1941, 30" x 53½", VG......$500.00

Cardboard, poster, vertical, "For the party," soldier and woman on bicycle for two, 29" x 50½", EX........$425.00

Cardboard, poster, vertical, "Happy Ending to Thirst," 1940s, 16" x 27", VG.......................................$250.00

Cardboard, poster, "Wherever thirst goes," great graphics of girl in row boat with a bucket of iced Coca-Cola, 1942, EX, $475.00.

Cardboard, poster, woman sitting wearing a broad brimmed hat with flowers, holding a Coca-Cola 5¢ bamboo fan and a glass, framed, 1912, EX, $4,500.00.

Cardboard poster, "Wherever you go," travel scenes in background, 1950s, EX, $175.00.

Cardboard, poster, vertical, "Have a Coke, Coca-Cola," couple at masquerade ball, framed under glass, rare item, F $550.00

Cardboard, poster, vertical, "Refreshment," pretty girl in fancy dress at a pool setting with bottles on table, 1949, 33½" x 54", VG $450.00

Cardboard poster, vertical, "Right off the ice," girl at ice skating rink, 1946, 16" x 27", EX..............$210.00

Cardboard, poster, vertical, "Start Refreshed," couple at roller skating rink, 1943, 16" x 27", VG $300.00

Cardboard, poster, vertical, "Thirst knows no season," couple building a snowman, graphics are great, 1942, 30" x 50", NM......................$700.00

Cardboard, poster, vertical, two sided, bottle on one side and target and bottle on the other side, French Canadian, 1951, EX $190.00

Cardboard, poster, vertical, with large bottle in foreground and places and events in background, "58 Million a Day," 1957, 17½" x 28½", F $75.00

Cardboard poster, vertical, "Play Refreshed," 1949, EX..................$750.00

Cardboard, promotional sign for cups featuring Sprite Boy, 1940s, 15" x 12", F, $350.00.

Cardboard, rack sign featuring Eddie Fisher on radio, 1954, 12" x 20", EX, $130.00.

Cardboard, sign featuring straight sided bottle "Demand the Genuine by Full Name, Nicknames Encourage Substitution," 1914, 30" x 18", F, $500.00.

Photos courtesy Muddy River Trading Co./Gary Metz

Cardboard, poster, "Yes," girl on beach with bottle, if found in original frame add $400.00 to this price, 1946, 56" x 27", EX $450.00

Cardboard, sign featuring girl with bowling ball, 1960s, 66" x 32", NM.............................$650.00

Cardboard six pack bottle display with motorized hand in bottle that moves up and down, "Take Enough Home," 1950s, EX $325.00

Cardboard, small vertical, "So refreshing" with woman in white spotlight, 1941, EX $750.00

Cardboard, sports favorite, hanging, complete set consists of 10 signs; individual signs go in the $85.00 – $110.00 range, 1947, EX ..$1,300.00

Cardboard, St. Louis Fair, woman sitting at table with a flare glass that has a syrup line, 1909, F ..$4,000.00

Cardboard, 3-D, "Boy oh Boy," pictures boy in front of cooler with a bottle in hand, 1937, 36" x 34", VG $800.00

Cardboard, 3-D cut-out sign featuring a sandwich and a glass, 1958, 17" x 20", F $55.00

Cardboard, trolley car sign, matted and framed, "Around the corner from anywhere," 1927, EX, $2,600.00.

Cardboard, trolley car sign, "Tired ?, Coca-Cola relieves fatigue," 1907, 20½" x 10¼", F, $2,300.00.

Cardboard, trolley car sign, "Relieves fatigue, Sold everywhere" good graphics, 1907, 20" x 10¼", F, $3,400.00.

Photos courtesy Muddy River Trading Co./Gary Metz

Cardboard, 3-D, "On Your Break," self-framing, 1950s, F $100.00

Cardboard, "Things go better with Coke" sign with gold frame, 1950s – 60s, 24" x 20", F ..$160.00

Cardboard, trolley car sign, "Delicious and Refreshing Drink Coca-Cola At Fountains Everywhere 5¢", 1905, 20½" x 10¾", F........$1,850.00

Cardboard, trolley car sign featuring a woman sitting off the side of hammock holding glass, 1912, EX $3,100.00

Cardboard, trolley sign, double long, "Yes," 1946, 28" x 11", NM....$750.00

Cardboard, trolley sign, "Drink Coca-Cola Delicious and Refreshing," 21" x 11", F......................................$675.00

Cardboard, truck poster, hard to find, girl in water, 1960s, 67" x 32", NM $120.00

Cardboard, truck poster, "Refreshing new feeling," 1960s, 67" x 32", EX $110.00

Cardboard, truck poster, "Yield to the Children," hard to find, NM ..$350.00

Cardboard, vertical poster featuring girl at water, 1938, 30" x 50", EX, $4,000.00.

Cardboard, two-sided die cut foldout sign featuring girl with glass "Be Really Refreshed," 1960s, 13" x 17", EX, $425.00.

Photos courtesy Muddy River Trading Co./Gary Metz

Cardboard, vertical double sided sign, "The best of taste" on one side "Enjoy the quality taste" on the other, 1956, 56" x 27", G $220.00

Cardboard, vertical, "For Holiday Entertaining," six bottle carton 36¢, featuring Christmas decor, Canadian, 1950, 12½" x 18½", EX ..$85.00

Cardboard, vertical poster featuring bathing beauty, great graphics, 1934, 29" x 50", EX $2,700.00

Cardboard, vertical poster featuring fishing girl, 1953, 16" x 27", EX $600.00

Cardboard, vertical poster featuring girl at beach, framed under glass, 1930s, G $1,150.00

Cardboard, vertical poster featuring girl on sidewalk, "So easy to carry home," 1942, 16" x 27", EX $800.00

Cardboard, vertical poster featuring girl standing beside a cooler with an umbrella, 1942, EX..............$475.00

Cardboard, vertical poster featuring girl with a tennis racquet, 1945, EX $500.00

Muddy River Trading Co./Gary Metz

Celluloid hanging "Highballs" sign, with original hanging chain, gold lettering on black background, 1921, 11¼" x 6", EX, $6,200.00.

Celluloid bottle, "Drink Coca-Cola Delicious and Refreshing," 1900, 6" x 13¼", VG, $1,800.00.

Celluloid disk, foreign, Spanish, rare, yellow and white on red, 1940s, 9", NM, $325.00.

Muddy River Trading Co./Gary Metz

Cardboard, vertical poster featuring girl with umbrella in front of cooler, "Talk about refreshing," 1942, 16" x 27", G $400.00

Cardboard, vertical poster featuring woman in yellow dress, walking in rain with an umbrella, 1942, G $375.00

Cardboard, vertical poster with a couple at "Coke Time" and a six pack in spotlight at bottom, 1943, EX $900.00

Cardboard, vertical poster with girl on ping pong table, framed under glass, Canadian, 14" x 28", EX $600.00

Cardboard, vertical, "So Refreshing," Autumn Girl in art work, 1940, 16" x 27", VG $425.00

Cardboard, "Welcome friend," red and white lettering on simulated oak background, 1957, 14" x 12", EX $135.00

Cardboard, window display, cameo fold out, 1913, VG $5,200.00

Cardboard, window display, die cut, depicting a circus, large center piece is 4' x 3', a separate girl and ring master are approx. 30" tall, three scenes, clown at big top, vendors and tents, ringmaster and girl, 1932, EX $4,600.00

Countertop light-up sign, "Drink Coca-Cola" with glass in spotlight at bottom center, back lit with red and white bulbs, manufactured by Brunhoff Mfg. Co., red and white, 1930s, 12" x 14", EX, $6,200.00.

Decal, "Drink Coca-Cola in Bottles," framed, 1950s, 15" x 9", NM, $45.00.

Die cut Coca-Cola bottle sign, 1951, 6' tall, G, $525.00.

Photos courtesy Muddy River Trading Co./Gary Metz

Cardboard, window display, trifold, Wallace Beery and Jackie Cooper sitting in director's chairs with a bottle in between them, 1934, 43" x 31½", VG $2,750.00

Celluloid over tin, "Refresh Yourself Drink Coca-Cola," probably manufactured in the U.S.A. for use in Canada, yellow & white on red with green frame, 1930s, 11¾" x 6", EX $1,800.00

Celluloid round, "Coca-Cola," white lettering on top of a bottle in center with red background, 1950s, 9" dia, EX......................................$175.00

Celluloid sign, "Delicious and Refreshing," red, 1940s, 9" dia, G $200.00

Coca-Cola fashion girl, one of four fashion girls, framed and under glass, 1932, EX $5,500.00

Decal, "Drink Coca-Cola Ice Cold," 1960, EX....................................$35.00

Decal for window, featuring bottle on blue background with original envelope, blue, 1940s, 8" x 13½", NM.......................................$35.00

Die cut bottle sign, 1953, 3' tall, NM.....................................$350.00

Festoon, five piece Square Dance back bar display with the original envelope, 1957, 18" x 11', G, $1,400.00.

Festoon, nine piece back bar display, hard to find, complete with original envelope and instruction card, 1958, 12' long, NM, $1,600.00.

Photos courtesy Muddy River Trading Co./Gary Metz

Die cut original artwork of boy with Coke glass, framed under glass, 1940s, 8" x14", EX $1,200.00

Dispenser sign featuring stainless band around border, red on white, 1950s, 27" x 28", EX $900.00

"Drink Coca-Cola, Cures Headache... Relieves Exhaustion at Soda Fountains 5¢," framed under glass, 1890 – 1900s, VG..............$1,000.00

Festoon, five piece back bar display, great graphics and very scarce, 1927, 11' long, EX $3,500.00

Festoon, three pieces of a five piece back bar display featuring girls' heads, 1951, F $700.00

Fountain service sign, two-sided, features early dispenser, red on yellow background, 1941, 25" x 26", NM $2,200.00

Glass and metal frame menu board with fishtail logo at top center, 1960s, 37" x 20", G $450.00

Glass and metal light-up, "work safely, work refreshed," cardboard insert, with original packing box, 1950s, 16" x 16", EX $675.00

Glass front light-up sign that has an illusion of movement, featuring "Have a Coke " arrow and a cup of Coke, hard-to-find item, 1950s, 17" x 10" x 3", NM, $1,400.00.

Illusion light-up sign, plastic front, 1960s, 11", NM, $775.00.

Light-up counter top "Pause" motion sign, with original box, 1950s, EX, $800.00.

Photos courtesy Muddy River Trading Co./Gary Metz

Glass framed sign featuring a bell shaped glass with diminishing logo at top, hard-to-find piece, 1930s, 6" x 9½", M..........................$2,000.00

Glass front light-up, "Please Pay When Served," located on top of courtesy panel, 1950s, 18" x 8", EX $550.00

Glass light-up, "Have A Coke, Refresh Yourself" with red arrow, 1950s, 10" x 17", NM........$1,200.00

Glass, round mirror, "Drink Carbonated Coca-Cola 5¢ in Bottles," G $400.00

Kay Displays sign "Quick Service" with die cut metal filigree, 1930s, 36" x 10", G.......................$2,100.00

Light-up "Beverage Department" with fishtail logo, 1960s, 50" x 14" ..$300.00

Light-up counter sign featuring 20 oz. bottle, NOS in original box, 1990s, 12" x 13", NM $190.00

Light-up counter top sign, "Please Pay When Served," red and white, 1948, 20' x 12", EX...........$2,800.00

Light-up counter sign with dispenser, 1959, 12'w x 27't x 15'd, G....$950.00

Light-up "Work Safely" plastic with cardboard insert and Coca-Cola paper cup on left of lower panel, 1950s, 15½" sq., G, $725.00.

Masonite, die cut sign with teenagers on records, hard to find, 1950s, 12", EX, $2,200.00.

Masonite, Kay Displays sign featuring a metal button in center of wings that have a Sprite Boy decal on each end, 1940s, 78" x 12", EX, $850.00.

Photos courtesy Muddy River Trading Co./Gary Metz

Light-up, plastic and glass, "Pause and Refresh," "Quality carries on" on right side with bottle in hand, same art work as appears on fans of this vintage, 1940s, 19" x 15½", EX..............$650.00

Light-up, plastic and metal display, "Always a Party, Always Coca-Cola," for Superbowl XXVII, NM $40.00

Light-up, plastic, rotating, "Shop Refreshed, Drink Coca-Cola," 1950s, 21" tall, G $525.00

Light-up, plastic with metal base, "Shop Refreshed," "Drink Coca-Cola," 1950s, EX $425.00

Masonite, "Delicious & Refreshing," girl with bottle, 1940s, EX $95.00

Masonite, diamond shaped "Drink Coca-Cola" sign with bottle in spot light at bottom, yellow and white on red background, 1946, 42" sq, NM $950.00

Masonite, horizontal, "Drink Coca-Cola Fountain Service," fountain heads on outside of lettering, 1930 – 40s, 27" x 14", EX.................$1,200.00

Masonite, Kay Displays sign featuring the silhouette girl, white on red, 1939, 17" dia, F......................$150.00

Metal, double sided fountain service sign, 1934, 23" x 26", NM, $1,600.00.

Muddy River Trading Co./Gary Metz

Metal, cooler panel insert, "Serve yourself, Please pay the Clerk," yellow & white on red, 1931, 31" x 11", G, $140.00.

Metal, double sided sidewalk sign, Canadian, 1949, 58" x 28", NM, $1,200.00.

Masonite, Sprite Boy in arrow through cooler, 1940s, EX ..$700.00

Metal, bag holder, painted, "For Home Refreshment Coca-Cola," Sprite Boy, 36" x 17", VG $400.00

Metal, button, 12", with wings, Sprite Boy on ends and lettering of Sundaes and Malts in between, 1950s, 12" x 78", VG $1,050.00

Metal, Canadian cartoon rack, features sign at top advertising "Take home a carton 30¢," 1930s, 5' tall, NM $450.00

Metal, die cut radiator script sign "Drink Coca-Cola In Bottles," 1920s, 17", EX......................$275.00

Metal, double sided, "In any weather Drink Coca-Cola," thermometer on one side fits on outside of screen door, while the "Thanks, Call Again" fits on the inside of the door, rare, 1930s, G $2,100.00

Metal, double sided sidewalk sign featuring an early dispenser, difficult to find, 1940s, 25' x 26", NM ..$2,500.00

Metal double sided sidewalk sign, 30" x 60", EX.......................$750.00

Muddy River Trading Co./Gary Metz

Metal, flange, Italian, American made sign, white & yellow on red, 1920s, 16" x 12", NM, $1,500.00.

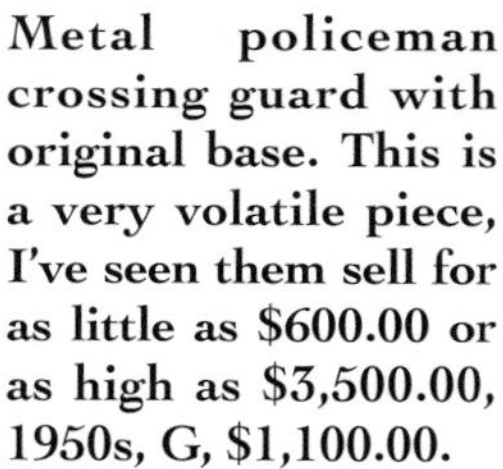

Metal policeman crossing guard with original base. This is a very volatile piece, I've seen them sell for as little as $600.00 or as high as $3,500.00, 1950s, G, $1,100.00.

Muddy River Trading Co./Gary Metz

Metal two-sided rack rack sign, "Serve Coca-Cola Sign of Good Taste," 1960s, 17" x 10", G, $95.00.

Metal, "Drink Coca-Cola, Delicious and Refreshing," bottle on left side, "The Icy-O Company Inc., Charlotte, N.C," EX $850.00

Metal, fishtail, painted "Drink Coca-Cola," white lettering on red, 1960s, 14" x 8", G 95.00

Metal, French Canadian sidewalk sign, "Buvez Coca-Cola," 1949, 58" x 28", EX $350.00

Metal, French Canadian carton rack, advertising 25¢ cartons, sign has French on one side and English on the reverse side, 1930s, 5' tall, EX..$400.00

Metal lollipop, "Drink Coca-Cola Refresh!," not on proper base, 1950s, G $495.00

Metal, sidewalk, "For Headache and Exhaustion Drink Coca-Cola," with 4" legs, manufactured by Ronemers & Co., Baltimore, Md., 1895 – 90, G $7,500.00

Neon script sign on two glass rods with the transformer hooked up in a separate location, red, 1930s, 27" x 12", EX $1,200.00

Neon, "Coca-Cola in bottles," great colors, metal base, 1950s, EX $1,200.00

Neon sign with original wrinkle paint, 1939, 17" x 13½", G, $1700.00.

Oil on canvas that has been dry mounted on board featuring soda jerk with glasses of Coke, back is marked Forbes litho, 1940s, 22" x 17", F, $2,300.00.

Original artwork of outdoor retail location, 1970s, 30" x 20", EX, $50.00.

Photos courtesy Muddy River Trading Co./Gary Metz

Neon, "Coke with Ice," three colors, 1980s, EX $350.00

Neon disk, "Drink...Sign of Good Taste," 1950s, 16" dia, EX....$500.00

Neon, "The Official Soft Drink of Summer," 1989, EX $1,100.00

Neon sign featuring three colors of girl drinking from can, yellow, red & pink, recent, 20" x 20", NM ..$180.00

Oil cloth, Lillian Nordica, "Coca-Cola at Soda Fountain 5¢," "Delicious Refreshing," rare, 1904, 25" x 47", EX $10,000.00

Original artwork depicting actors taking a break from work on a western movie, signed by Verne Tossey, 1950s, 22" x 14", NM........$1,000.00

Paper advertising, "See adventures of Kit Carson," 1953, 24" x 16", EX..$85.00

Paper, bottler's calendar advance print, Garden Girl on a golf course, framed under glass, rare, 1919, NM.......................$7,500.00

Paper, China girl sitting with a glass of Coke, matted and framed, 1936, 14¼" x 22", NM $1,800.00

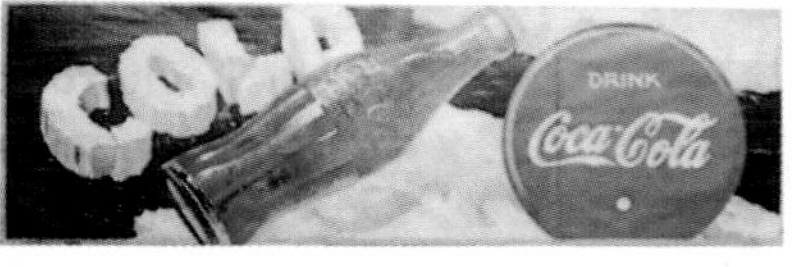

Muddy River Trading Co./Gary Metz

Paper poster featuring a bottle of Coke on snow, printed on heavy outdoor paper, 1942, 57" x 18", EX, $130.00.

Muddy River Trading Co./Gary Metz

Paper poster featuring man and woman with flared glasses and the globe motif, 1912, 38" x 49", F, $16,500.00.

Paper poster, horizontal, "Let's have a Coke," couple in uniform, 1930s, 57" x 20", G, $850.00.

Paper, "Drink Coca-Cola Delicious and Refreshing," bottle in front of hot dog, framed and under glass, EX $150.00

Paper, "Drink Coca-Cola, Quick Refreshment," bottle in front of hot dog, framed under glass, EX .. $150.00

Paper, Edgar Bergen and Charlie McCarthy, CBS Sunday Evenings, 1949, 22" x 11", EX $165.00

Paper, Gibson Girl, matted and framed, if in mint condition price would go to about $4,000.00, 1910, 20" x 30", F $2,500.00

Paper, girl in white dress with large red bow in back with a bottle and a straw, matted and framed under glass. There are two versions of this, the other one is identical except the waist bow is pink, 1910s, F $2,500.00

Paper, girl sitting on slat back bench wearing a large white hat with a red ribbon and drinking from a bottle with a straw, framed, 1913, 16" x 24", G $4,000.00

Paper poster featuring flapper girl with a bottle of Coke, 1920s, 12" x 2", G $400.00

Paper poster "Refresh," on heavy outdoor paper, 1940s, 57" x 18", EX, $275.00.

Paper poster "Treat yourself right" featuring man with a sandwich opening a bottle of Coke, 1920s, 12" x 20", F, $550.00.

Paper, window display, die cut, glass shaped, "Drink Coca-Cola," rare, 12" x 20", EX, $1,800.00.

Photos courtesy Muddy River Trading Co./Gary Metz

Paper poster, "Ritz Boy," first time Ritz Boy was used, framed under glass, 1920s, F $500.00

Paper poster, vertical, "Drink Coca-Cola Delicious and Refreshing," matted, framed under glass, 1927 – 28, 12" x 20", VG..................$475.00

Paper poster, vertical, "Pause a minute Refresh yourself," roll down with top and bottom metal strips, 1927 – 28, 12" x 20", EX ..$1,800.00

Paper, Sprite Boy, "Come In, Have a Coke," framed under glass, EX $150.00

Paper "That taste-good feeling," boy with Coca-Cola and hot dog, 1920s, EX $650.00

Paper, two women drinking from bottles sitting in front of an ocean scene with clouds in the sky, 1912, 16" x 22", VG $4,000.00

Paper, "which" Coca-Cola or Goldelle Ginger Ale, this one has been trimmed with lettering eliminated, framed and under glass, 1905, G.............$3,000.00

Paper window set for bottle sales, three piece, "Home Refreshment," 1941, 31" tall, G....................$200.00

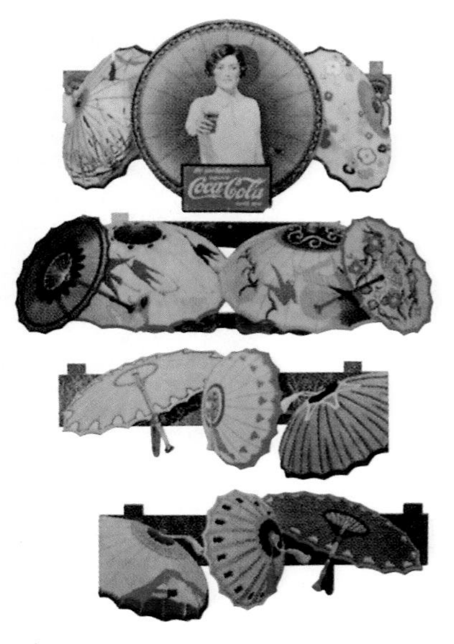

Parasols, five piece festoon, originally placed on a soda fountain back bar, 1927, G, $4,700.00.

Plywood, Kay Displays triangle with down arrow, 24" x 26", G, $500.00.

Photos courtesy Muddy River Trading Co./Gary Metz

Paper window sign, "Let Us Put A Case In Your Car," case of Coca-Cola, 36" x 20", EX $230.00

Plastic and metal light-up die cut sign, shaped like a paper serving cup, 1950-60s, 16" x 17", G $1,300.00

Plastic, "Delicious With Ice Cold Coca-Cola," popcorn box overflowing with popcorn, 24" x 7", EX $35.00

Plastic front light-up sign that gives a movement illusion when lit, "Drink Coca-Cola In Bottles" in red center, 1960s, 11" dia, EX....$675.00

Plastic hanging light-up sign, "Leo's Fountain," 1950s, 24" x 28", EX....................................$425.00

Plastic light-up, "Work Safely," "Safety is a job" cardboard insert, shows a Coca-Cola paper cup in lower left, 1950s, 15½" sq, EX $775.00

Plywood and metal, Kay Displays sign, black lettering on yellow background, 1930s, 37' x 10', G $1,550.00

Plywood, double sided, "Slow School Zone Enjoy Coca-Cola, Drive Safely," 1950 – 60s, EX $950.00

Plywood and metal arrow and bottle sign "Drink Coca-Cola Ice Cold," 1939, 17" dia, G, $400.00.

Plywood, triangle die cut sign with down arrow, "Ice Cold Drink Coca-Cola," Kay Displays, 1930s, EX, $750.00.

Porcelain, "Buvez Coca-Cola," with Sprite Boy in spotlight, French, 1940s, 58" x 18", EX, $750.00.

Photos courtesy Muddy River Trading Co./Gary Metz

Porcelain bottle button, 3' dia, M $550.00

Porcelain bottle, die cut, 1940s, 12", VG $100.00

Porcelain button "Drink Coca-Cola" considered to be the plain version of this piece, white on red, 1950s, 24", NM $375.00

Porcelain button "Drink Coca-Cola in Bottles," white on red, 1950s, 24", NM $425.00

Porcelain button with bottle only, white, 1950s, 24", NM $750.00

Porcelain button with bottle, "Coca-Cola," red, 24", NM $550.00

Porcelain button with bottle, white on red, 1950s, 48" dia, G......$225.00

Porcelain, "Buvez Coca-Cola," French Canadian sign, 1956, 29" x 12", EX ....$120.00.

Porcelain, Canadian button with flat edge, "Drink Coca-Cola Ice Cold," 1940s, 3' dia, G $165.00

Porcelain, Canadian "Coca-Cola Sold Here Ice Cold," white & yellow on red, 1947, 29" x 12", G....$200.00

Porcelain, Canadian "Drink Coca-Cola," 1946, 28" x 20", EX, $220.00.

Porcelain, Canadian fountain service sign, 1935, 27" x 14", NM, $1,200.00.

Porcelain, "Delicious, Refreshing" with bottle in center, 1950s, 24" sq, EX, $275.00.

Photos courtesy Muddy River Trading Co./Gary Metz

Porcelain, Canadian "Drink Coca-Cola" button, 1954, 4' dia, NM............$475.00

Porcelain, Canadian "Drink Coca-Cola" sign, red, yellow, and white, 1955, 29" x 12", EX..............$250.00

Porcelain, Canadian flange "Iced Coca-Cola Here," 1952, 18" x 20", NM $575.00

Porcelain, Canadian fountain service sign, 1937, 8' x 4', NM $1,800.00

Porcelain, "Come In! Have A Coca-Cola," yellow and white, 1940s, 54", NM $1,100.00

Porcelain, "Delicious & Refreshing," white background, 1950s, 24" x 24", EX $275.00

Porcelain, delivery truck cab, "Ice Cold," red, white, and yellow, arched top, 1930s, NM........$700.00

Porcelain, die cut bottle sign, 1950s, 16" tall, EX $260.00

Porcelain, die cut bottle sign, 12' tall, G $150.00

Porcelain, die cut script "Drink Coca-Cola" sign, white, 18" x 5½", M $775.00

Porcelain, double sided flange sign "Drink Coca-Cola Here," 1940s, NM, $850.00.

Porcelain, fishtail sign with turned ends, "Drink Coca-Cola," white on red, 1950s, 44" x 16", M, $275.00.

Porcelain, "Drink Coca-Cola" shield sign, white & yellow on red, 1942, 3' x 2', F, $225.00.

Photos courtesy Muddy River Trading Co./Gary Metz

Porcelain, double sided, "Drink Coca-Cola" on one side, "Isenhower Cigar Store" on other side, 1930, 30" x 40", G $200.00

Porcelain, double-sided lunch sign, 1950s, 28" x 25", NM........$1,500.00

Porcelain, "Drink Coca-Cola, Ice Cold," fountain dispenser, 1950s, 28" x 28", EX $500.00

Porcelain, "Drink Coca-Cola in bottles" sign with curved ends, white lettering on red, 1950s, 44" x 16", EX $90.00

Porcelain, "Drink Coca-Cola" on fishtail, 1950 – 60s, 44" x 16", NM..$275.00

Porcelain, "Drink Coca-Cola" sign, 1910s, 45" x 18", EX..........$1,000.00

Porcelain, "Drug Store" over "Drink Coca-Cola Delicious & Refreshing," red, white, and green, 1930s, 90" x 60", EX $625.00

Porcelain, "Drugs, Soda," 1950s, 18" x 30", NM $950.00

Porcelain, flange "Drink" sign, Canadian, yellow and white on red, 1930s, 17" x 20", EX $475.00

Porcelain, flange, "Have a Coca-Cola," 1951, 17" x 19", EX, $400.00.

Porcelain, French Canadian flange sign, "Buvez Coca-Cola Glace," 1950s, 18" x 19", NM, $200.00.

Porcelain, flange "Refresh Yourself, Coca-Cola Sold Here Ice Cold" on shield shaped sign, 1930s, 17" x 20", G, $525.00.

Photos courtesy Muddy River Trading Co./Gary Metz

Porcelain, flange, "Enjoy Coca-Cola In Bottles," very rare and hard to find, 1948, EX $850.00

Porcelain, flange French Canadian, "Prenez un Coca-Cola," 1950s, 17" x 19", EX $200.00

Porcelain, fountain service, "Drink Coca-Cola Fountain Service," white and yellow lettering on red and black background framed by fountain heads, 27" x 14", EX ..$1,200.00

Porcelain, "Fountain Service, Drink Coca-Cola" on button, 1950s, 34" x 12", NM $400.00

Porcelain, fountain service sign, "Fountain Service, Drink Coca-Cola," red, green, white, 1950s, 28" x 12", EX $800.00

Porcelain, fountain service sign, 1935, 27" x 14", NM..........$1,800.00

Porcelain, French Canadian door kick plate, 1939, 29" x 12", NM $210.00

Porcelain, French Canadian double sided flange sign, 1940, EX ..$500.00

Porcelain, French Canadian sidewalk sign, both message and legs are porcelain, 1941, 27" x 46", EX $250.00

Porcelain, French Canadian sign, because of its construction it resembles the smaller door push, 1930s, 18" x 54", G, $400.00.

Porcelain, outdoor advertising sign, "Drug Store, Drink Coca-Cola, Delicious and Refreshing," red, white, and green, 1933, 5' x 3'6", EX, $1,100.00.

Porcelain, sidewalk sign and legs, double sided, "Stop Here Drink Coca-Cola," 1941, 27" x 46", F, $225.00.

Photos courtesy Muddy River Trading Co./Gary Metz

Porcelain, French Canadian sign, "Buvez Coca-Cola," white, red, & yellow, 1955, 29" x 12", G....$100.00

Porcelain, horizontal, "Coca-Cola Sold Here Ice Cold," red background trimmed in yellow with white lettering, 1940s, 29" x 12", G.....................$90.00

Porcelain, outdoor, "Drink Coca-Cola Delicious and Refreshing," white and yellow lettering on red background, 1938, 8' x 4', NM $1,300.00

Porcelain, horizontal, "Drink Coca-Cola Fountain Service," yellow background, 1950s, 28" x 12", EX ..$700.00

Porcelain, kick plate for screen door "Drink Coca-Cola Sold Here Ice Cold," 1930s, 31" x 12", G....$425.00

Porcelain, round bottle unit, probably part of a larger sign, features the 1923 bottle, 18", NM............$225.00

Porcelain, sidewalk, double sided vertical, "Stop Here Drink Coca-Cola," Canadian, 1941, 26" x 36", EX $325.00

Porcelain, square sign featuring button in center, Italian, 22" sq, NM $525.00

Porcelain, truck sign , "Drink Coca-Cola Ice Cold," yellow & white lettering on red, 1940s, 50" x 10", G, $130.00.

Reverse glass with original chain and frame, "Drink Coca-Cola," rare version in red, white lettering on red background, 1932, 20" x 12", EX, $3,500.00.

Starburst light-up with Coca-Cola bottle in center "Drink Coca-Cola" fish-tail at bottom, 1960s, 14" x 16", EX, $500.00.

Reverse painted glass, "Refresh Yourself Drink Coca-Cola," Canadian, 1927, 11½" x 5½", G, $325.00.

Photos courtesy Muddy River Trading Co./Gary Metz

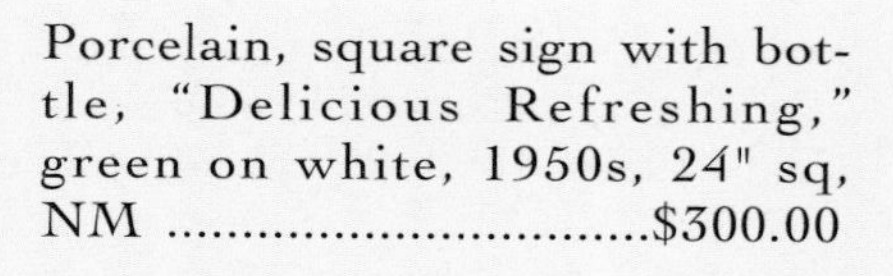

Porcelain, square sign with bottle, "Delicious Refreshing," green on white, 1950s, 24" sq, NM $300.00

Porcelain, 24" button "Drink Coca-Cola, Sign of Good Taste," white lettering on red, 1950s, 24", NM $400.00

Reverse glass, "Drink Coca-Cola," 1920s, 10" x 6", EX...........$1,200.00

Reverse glass, "Drink Coca-Cola," for back bar mirror, 1930s, 11" dia, EX $525.00

Rice paper napkin with girl and bottle with arrow, framed and matted under glass, EX.....................$50.00

Rice paper napkin with Oriental scene, VG.............................$350.00

Tin, arrow, "Ice Cold Coca-Cola Sold Here," white lettering on red and green background, 30", G $200.00

Tin, bottle, oval, "Drink A Bottle of Carbonated Coca-Cola," rare, 1900s, 8½" x 10½", EX $7,500.00

Tin, bottle sign with original wooden frame, 1950s, 18" x 36", EX ..$170.00

Tin, button with Sprite Boy decal, white, 1950s, 16", NM, $775.00.

Tin, Canadian sign featuring 6 oz. bottle on right, 1930s, 28" x 20", G, $325.00.

Tin, Canadian six pack in spotlight "Take home a carton," 1940, 36" x 60", G, $200.00.

Photos courtesy Muddy River Trading Co./Gary Metz

Tin, bottle sign with original wooden frame, 1948, 18" x 36", G......$150.00

Tin, button with circle and earlier arrow, with framework on back, red & white, 1953, 12" dia, EX ..$475.00

Tin, button with large arrow and original connecting hardware, red on white, 16" dia, NM...............$500.00

Tin, Canadian "Drink Coca-Cola Ice Cold," 1938, 5' x 3', G $400.00

Tin, Canadian "Drink Coca-Cola" sign, G, bright colors, 1956, 28" x 20", EX $450.00

Tin, Canadian six pack in spotlight "Take home a carton," 1940, 36" x 60", G $200.00

Tin, Canadian six pack in spotlight, "Take home a carton," 1942, 18" x 54", EX $500.00

Tin, Canadian vertical "Refresh yourself" sign with 6 oz. bottle, 1920s, 18" x 54", G $600.00

Tin, "Candy-Cigarettes" over fishtail logo, self-framed, 1960s, 28" x 20", EX..$225.00

Tin, die cut bottle sign, 1932, 12" x 39", G, $550.00.

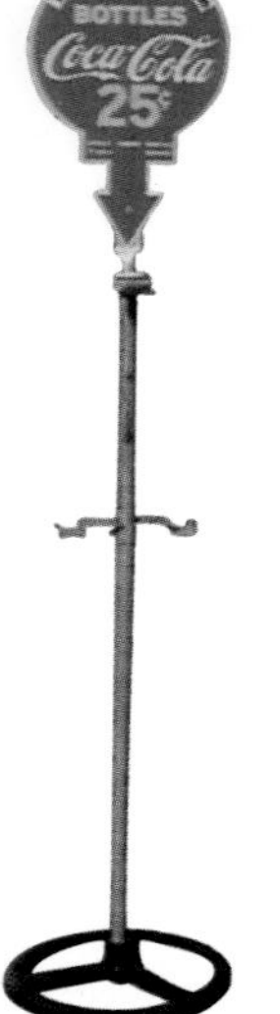

Tin, carton rack with great rare sign at top, hard to find this one, 1930s, 5' tall, NM, $825.00.

Tin, die cut six pack sign, featuring carrier with handle, advertising 6 for 25¢, 1950, 11" x 13", EX, $775.00.

Photos courtesy Muddy River Trading Co./Gary Metz

Tin, "Cold Drinks," 1960s, 24" x 15", NM $200.00

Tin, "Cold Drinks" with "Drink" fishtail, "With Crushed Ice," 1960s, 24" x 15", NM $225.00

Tin, "Cold Drinks" with fishtail in center, 1960s, 24" x 15", NM $200.00

Tin, diamond shaped, with bottle spotlighted at bottom, in original black wooden frame, "Drink Coca-Cola" at top, 1940, 42" x 42", NM $500.00

Tin, die cut bottle sign, 1930s, 39" tall, G $550.00

Tin, die cut bottle sign, 1949, 20" x 72", NM $625.00

Tin, die cut bottle sign, 1951, 16" tall, G $140.00

Tin, die cut fishtail "Coca-Cola" sign, white on red, 1962, 24" x 12", NM $425.00

Tin, die cut fishtail sign "Coca-Cola," white on red, 1962, 26" x 12", NM $500.00

Tin, die cut six pack sign, 6 for 25¢, 1950s, 11" x 13", EX $600.00

Tin, die cut 12 pack sign, 1954, 20" x 14", NM, $1,700.00.

Tin, double sided arrow sign "Coca-Cola Sold Here Ice Cold," red, green & white, 1927, F, $300.00.

Tin, double sided flange fishtail sign, red on white and green, 1960s, 18" x 15", G, $300.00.

Photos courtesy Muddy River Trading Co./Gary Metz

Tin, die cut triangle sign with the original bracket and mounting hardware, 1934, EX..................$1,750.00

Tin, door kickplate sign, "Drink Coca-Cola" with bottle in spotlight, yellow & white on red, 1946, 34" x 11", EX $175.00

Tin, double sided rack sign, "Take home a Carton," yellow, white on red, 1930s, 13", G $200.00

Tin, double sided triangle "Ice Cold" with bottle at bottom, filigree work at top, 1936, 23" x 23", F $675.00

Tin, "Drink" button with '40s style arrow attachment at back of fixture with original hardware, 1948, 16", NM $900.00

Tin, "Drink..." button with wings, 1950s, 32" x 12", NM $275.00

Tin,"Drink Coca-Cola," American Artworks with scalloped top and filigree, 1936, EX $850.00

Tin, "Drink Coca-Cola" button with small arrow and original hardware, white on red, 1950s, 12" dia, EX $475.00

Tin, "Drink Coca-Cola Ice Cold" in red arrow pointing right at bottle in white background, red & white, 1952, 27" x 19", NM, $250.00.

Tin, "Drink Coca-Cola Ice Cold," 1923 with embossed bottle at left, note shadow on bottle, 1937, 28" x 20", G, $525.00.

Tin, "Drink Coca-Cola" sign with marching bottles, note shadow on bottles, 1937, 54" x 18", NM, $800.00.

Photos courtesy Muddy River Trading Co./Gary Metz

Tin, "Drink Coca-Cola" button with small arrow, 1950s, 12" dia, F $175.00

Tin, "Drink Coca-Cola Delicious & Refreshing," couple with a bottle, 1940s, 28" x 20", EX $550.00

Tin, "Drink Coca-Cola 5¢ Ice Cold," self framing, tilted bottle, 1930s, 54" x 18", EX $350.00

Tin, "Drink Coca-Cola In Bottles" button with arrow shooting from right to left at about 2 and 8 o'clock, 1954, EX $325.00

Tin, "Drink Coca-Cola" lettered in white over dynamic wave logo, 1980s, 24" x 18", EX $40.00

Tin, "Drink Coca-Cola Sign of Good Taste," white and yellow on red, 1950s, 12" dia, EX $250.00

Tin, "Drink Coca-Cola," 24" iron frame, one side has a 16" button while the opposite side as a 10" plastic button with a small light which creates a back light, VG $975.00

Tin, embossed, "Drink Coca-Cola Delicious and Refreshing," 14" x 10", F $210.00

Tin, raised frame "Drink" sign with 1923 bottle, 1942, 28" x 20", G, $550.00.

Tin, embossed "Gas Today" with spotlight blackboard in center, 1936, 18" x 54", G, $700.00.

Tin, embossed "Ice Cold Coca-Cola Sold Here," featuring 1916 bottle, 1926, 28" x 20", F, $200.00.

Tin, embossed sign "Drink Coca-Cola on Bottles 5¢," white lettering on red, 1920s, 23" x 6", EX, $450.00.

Photos courtesy Muddy River Trading Co./Gary Metz

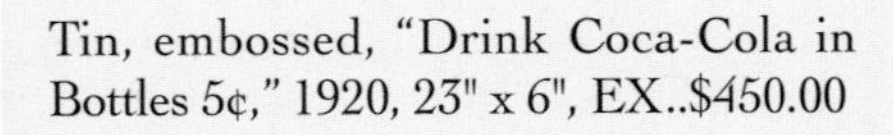

Tin, embossed, "Drink Coca-Cola in Bottles 5¢," 1920, 23" x 6", EX..$450.00

Tin, embossed "Drink Coca-Cola In Bottles 5¢ " sign, red & white, 1930s, 23" x 6", EX $275.00

Tin, embossed "Drink" sign by Dasco, in original wrapping paper, 1930s, 18" x 6", NM $350.00

Tin, embossed "Drink" sign with 1923 bottle on left side of sign,, 1931, 27½" x 10", NM $1,600.00

Tin, embossed "Gas Today" sign with good colors, 1929, 28" x 20", G..$650.00

Tin, embossed, "Ice Cold Coca-Cola Sold Here," green and white trim, 1933, 19½" dia, EX $475.00

Tin, embossed "Ice Cold Coca-Cola Sold Here," yellow & white on red, 1932, 29" x 19", F $375.00

Tin, embossed over cardboard with string holder, "Drink Coca-Cola," 1922, 8" x 4", EX..................$900.00

Tin, embossed sign featuring 1915 bottle, 1927, F $325.00

Tin, embossed sign featuring the 1923 bottle, 1920s, 28" x 20", F $275.00

Tin, fishtail sign "Drink Coca-Cola," horizontal, white lettering on red, 12" x 6", NM, $160.00.

Tin, flange bottle logo, rare and somewhat difficult to find, "enjoy Coca-Cola In Bottles," 1950s, 18", G, $475.00.

Tin, flange, "Drink Coca-Cola" with bottle in spotlight at lower corner, 1947, 24" x 20", G, $550.00.

Photos courtesy Muddy River Trading Co./Gary Metz

Tin, "Enjoy Coca-Cola All the Year Round," with giant earth, 1982, 33" x 24", EX $110.00

Tin, featuring artwork of straight sided bottle on left side of sign, 1914, 27" x 19", G.............$1,700.00

Tin, featuring Elaine holding a glass, 1916, 20" x 30", VG $5,000.00

Tin, fishtail die-cut, 1960s, 12" x 26", EX $250.00

Tin, fishtail flange, "Enjoy that Refreshing New Feeling," 1962, 18" x 15", EX $230.00

Tin, fishtail, horizontal, "Sign of the Good Taste," full-color bottle at right side of sign, all on white background with green trim on frame, 1959, 54" x 18", NM $250.00

Tin, fishtail sign with bottle on left and 12 oz. can on right, red, white, and green, 54" x 18", EX......$300.00

Tin, fishtail, vertical, "Drink Coca-Cola" with bottle at bottom of sign, 1960, 18" x 54", NM $230.00

Tin, flange, "Drink Coca-Cola," 1941, 24" x 21", EX..............$450.00

Tin, flange with filigree at top of piece, 1936, 20" x 13", EX, $700.00.

Tin, flat "Refresh yourself," sign "Drink Coca-Cola Sold Here Ice Cold," yellow & white on red, 1927, 28" x 29", G, $350.00.

Tin, French six pack in spotlight, 1940s, 36" x 60", F, $140.00.

Photos courtesy Muddy River Trading Co./Gary Metz

Tin, French "Buvez" sign featuring Sprite Boy in spotlight on right side, 1948, 54" x 18", NM $850.00

Tin, French Canadian bottle sign, with 1916 bottle, 1920s, 28" x 20", F $150.00

Tin, French Canadian sign featuring 6 oz. bottle on right side, 1930s, 28" x 20", G $700.00

Tin, French, six pack in spotlight, 1942, 18" x 52", F $140.00

Tin, girl with glass, gold beveled edge, 1920s, 8" x 11", EX $875.00

Tin, "Grocery" over bottle with fishtail logo, 1960s, 28" x 20", G ..$100.00

Tin, heavy embossed,1923 bottle at each end, "Drink Coca-Cola" in center in white on red background, 1930s, EX $425.00

Tin, Hilda Clark, considered rare due to the fact this art work is rarely found in the tin version, 1903, 16¼"x19½", EX $3,700.00

Tin, Hilda Clark, round, "Coca-Cola Drink Delicious and Refreshing," very rare and hard to find piece, 1903, 6" dia, EX $5,000.00

Tin horizontal "Drink Coca-Cola" with bottle to right, red & white, 1954, 54" x 18", EX, $170.00.

Tin, horizontal "Enjoy Coca-Cola" with bottle to right of message in white square, red & white, 1960s, 54" x 18", NM, $200.00.

Tin, "Ice Cold Coca-Cola Sold Here," yellow & white on red, 1933, 20" dia, G, $225.00.

Photos courtesy Muddy River Trading Co./Gary Metz

Tin, Hilda Clark, showing her drinking from a glass while seated at a table with roses and stationery, very rare, 1899, VG ....$15,000.00.

Tin, horizontal, "Drink Coca-Cola," red background, silver border on self frame, bottle in spotlight in lower right hand corner, 1946, 28" x 20", EX........$340.00

Tin, horizontal embossed, "Drink Coca-Cola," 1923 bottle on left side, 35" x 12", EX $350.00

Tin, horizontal, "Things go better with Coke," self framing, 1960s, 32" x 12", NM..$180.00

Tin, "Ice Cold" featuring '60s cup, white on blue, 1960s, 28" x 20", NM $50.00

Tin, "It's A Natural! Coca-Cola In Bottles," over bottle on red background, 1950s, 16" dia, EX..$375.00

Tin, Kay Displays sign, cardboard back plate, stand up featuring "Drink Coca-Cola," 1930s, 9" x 10", EX $650.00

Tin, Lillian Nordica, oval framed, "Coca-Cola Delicious and Refreshing," featuring Coca-Cola table and oval "Drink Coca-Cola 5¢," rare, 1904, 8½" x 10¼", EX $7,500.00

Tin "Now Enjoy Coca-Cola at home," featuring hand carrying cardboard, six pack, rare and hard to find, Canadian sign, 1930s, 18" x 54", F, $1,050.00.

Tin, "Pause" sign with bottle in spotlight, 1940, 18" x 54", NM, $1,200.00.

Tin, pilaster sign, featuring bottle with 16" button at top of unit, 1948, 16" x 54", NM, $550.00.

Photos courtesy Muddy River Trading Co./Gary Metz

Tin, Lillian Nordica, self framed, embossed, promoting both fountain and bottle sales, 1904 – 05, EX $7,000.00

Tin, octagonal, "Drink Coca-Cola" over bottle in circle, 1930s, 10" dia, EX $500.00

Tin over cardboard, featuring a straight sided bottle, rare and hard to find, white background, 1908, 6" x 13", F $1,250.00

Tin, over cardboard, with "Drink Coca-Cola," featuring 1915 bottle, red lettering on white background, 1920s, 6" x 13", G $1,400.00

Tin, painted litho, "Drink Coca-Cola In Bottles 5¢," bottle on each side, framed, 1907, 34½" x 12", F $400.00

Tin, painted, "Take a case home today, $1.00 deposit," 19½" x 27¾", VG $100.00

Tin, "Pause Drink Coca-Cola," white lettering on red and yellow background, vertical, 1930s, 18" x 54", EX $220.00

Tin, pilaster sign, with six pack artwork and 16" button at top, 1948, 16" x 54", EX.......................$650.00

Tin, self-framing new Betty, "Drink Coca-Cola" sign, yellow & white on red, 1940, 28" x 20", F, $225.00.

Tin, sidewalk sign "Drink Coca-Cola Ice Cold, Delicious and Refreshing," yellow, white, red, and green, 1939, 20" x 28", NM, $275.00.

Tin, shadow bottle "Ice Cold" sign, hard to find, 1936, 18" x 54", G, $600.00.

Photos courtesy Muddy River Trading Co./Gary Metz

Tin, rack sign with Sprite Boy decal, yellow on red, 1940s, 16" x 23", EX $300.00

Tin, "Refresh Yourself, Drink Coca-Cola, Sold Here Ice Cold," 1927, 29" x 30", G $150.00

Tin, ribbon, die cut, "Sign of Good Taste," 1957, 3', NM $210.00

Tin, round sign with bottle and logo, red, 1937, 46", NM............$1,000.00

Tin, self-framing "Drink" sign with couple holding bottle, woman in spotlight, 1942, 28" x 20", EX $550.00

Tin, self-framing, horizontal oval, "Coca-Cola," girl in foreground of lettering offering a bottle, 1926, 11" x 8", F..................................$200.00

Tin, "Serve Coca-Cola At Home," yellow dot six pack, 1950s, 54" x 18", NM..............................$250.00

Tin, sidewalk sign "Big King Size" featuring fishtail over bottle all on green and white background, 1960s, 20" x 28", EX.......................$120.00

Tin, sidewalk sign "Delicious and refreshing," 1930s, 20" x 28", F..............................$125.00

Tin, sidewalk sign featuring 24 bottle case "Take a case home today," 1957, EX, $200.00.

Tin, six pack die cut sign with spotlight on carton, hard to find, 1958, 11" x 12", NM, $1,500.00.

Tin, six pack sign featuring six pack, "Take home a Carton," with fishtail "Coca-Cola" at top of sign, 1958, 20" x 28", EX, $550.00.

Photos courtesy Muddy River Trading Co./Gary Metz

Tin, sidewalk sign featuring fishtail over bottle on green and white striped background, 1960s, NM $170.00

Tin, sign featuring straight sided bottle with wooden frame, 1914, 28" x 20", P....................$225.00

Tin, "Sign of Good Taste" button, white & yellow on red, 1950s, 12" dia, F $125.00

Tin, "Sign of Good Taste" in fishtail with bottle at bottom on green and white striped background, 1960s, 16" x 41", EX....................$275.00

Tin, sign with man and woman in spotlight "Drink Coca-Cola," 1942, 56" x 32", NM $525.00

Tin, sign with woman with a bottle of Coca-Cola, "Drink Coca-Cola," 1942, 56" x 32", EX....................$475.00

Tin, six pack, die cut, "King Size, Coca-Cola," 1960s, EX....................$300.00

Tin, six pack, die cut, "6 for 25¢," 1950s, EX $500.00

Tin, "Take Home A Carton" over six pack, Canadian, 1950s, 53" x 35", NM $575.00

Tin, two-sided die cut arrow sign "Ice Cold Coca-Cola Sold Here," 1927, 30" x 8", G, $375.00.

Tin, "things go better" sign featuring "Drink" paper cup, hard to find, red, green, and white, 1960s, 28" x 20", NM, $600.00.

Tin, vertical "Pause" sign featuring bottle in spotlight in center, 1940, 18" x 54", F, $185.00.

Trolley car sign, matted and framed, "Four Seasons," 1923, 20¼" x 10¼", NM, $4,000.00.

Photos courtesy Muddy River Trading Co./Gary Metz

Tin, "Take Home a Carton," self-framing border, Canadian, 1950, 35" x 53", EX $625.00

Tin, "Take Home a Carton" sign, with six pack featured artwork, 1954, 20" x 28", NM $600.00

Tin, "Things Go Better With Coke" on right, with disk logo at left, 1960s, 21" x 11", EX $250.00

Tin, "Things Go Better With Coke" with bottle, disk logo on both sides raised border, 1960s, 54" x 18", EX...................$225.00

Tin, twelve pack, die cut, 1954, 20" x 13", NM $550.00

Tin, vertical "Enjoy that Refreshing new taste" in fishtail with bottle at bottom on green & white stripe background, 1960s, 16" x 41", NM..$325.00

Tin, vertical "Gas Today" sign, 1931, 18" x 54", G.......................$1,300.00

Tin, vertical "Gas Today" sign, 1937, 18" x 54", E.......................$1,600.00

Window decal, "Drink Coca-Cola" with fret work top, 1940, 25" x 12", M $110.00

Wood and masonite Kay Displays, sign advertising Sundaes and Malts with 12" button in center and Sprite Boy on each end, 1950s, 6'6" x 1', EX, $1,050.00.

Wood finish with chrome accents "Thirst asks nothing more," difficult to locate this piece, 38" x 10", G, $775.00.

Wood and wire, Kay Displays sign with bowling scene, 1940s, 16" dia, EX, $350.00.

Photos courtesy Muddy River Trading Co./Gary Metz

Wood and masonite, "Beverage Department" with Sprite Boy, 1950s, NM $1,200.00

Wood and masonite, hanging, "Drink Coca-Cola. Delicious... Refreshing," with silhouette on left-hand side, 1941, 3' x 1', NM $950.00

Wood and masonite, Kay Displays, refreshed communication sign, 1940s, EX $200.00

Wood, figural, die cut, "Coca-Cola" cooler, probably part of another sign, 1950s, EX $260.00

Wood, "Here's Refreshment," bottle and horseshoe on plank, 1940s, EX $325.00

Wood, Kay Displays, "Please Pay Cashier," filigree on ends, 1930s, 22" x 12", EX $1,500.00

Wood, Kay Displays sign, "Take some home today" double sided with button in center, 1940s, 3' x 1', F $550.00

Wood, Silhouette Girl, metal hanger, 1940, EX.......................... $450.00

Wood, Sprite Boy Welcome Friend, 1940, 32" x 14", EX $550.00

Wooden, hand painted, truck sign double sided with the maker's name on one side, with original metal brackets, "Every Bottle Sterilized," white lettering on red background, 1920s, 10' x 1', F, $425.00.

Wooden, three piece set manufactured by Kay Displays, 1930s, 37" x 10" center, 9" x 11½" end pieces, NM, $2,800.00.

Wooden, three piece Kay Displays made of plywood and metal, featuring embossed icicles, displayed at Weidelich Pharmacies until it closed in the early 1960s, 1936, 36" x 20" center, 36" x 18" end pieces, G, $4,000.00.

Photos courtesy Muddy River Trading Co./Gary Metz

Wooden, Kay Displays sign "Please Pay Cashier" on two bars above "Drink" display, 1930s, 22" x 12½", G $1,950.00

Wooden, Kay Displays sign with metal filigree at top with artwork of glasses in center, 1930s, 9" x 11½", NM $900.00

Wooden, Kay Displays, "While Shopping" with metal filigree at top and bottom, 1930s, 36" x 10", EX $1,500.00

Wooden, outdoor sign, weathered and worn advertising supplies, red and white on green, 1910s, 38" x 90", F......$150.00

Wood, "Quick Service" on board with red "Drink Coca-Cola" emblem below, 1930s, 10" x 3" EX....$2,000.00

Wood, Silhouette Girl, metal hanger, 1940, EX..........................$450.00

Wood, Sprite Boy Welcome Friend, 1940, 32" x 14", EX $550.00

Wood, "Yes," swimming girl miniature billboard, EX................$115.00

Wooden, School Zone sign, one side has silhouette girl running, other side has bottle over button, 1957, 16" x 48", EX $1,950.00

Calendar top, missing the bottom pad area, 1909, 11" x 14", EX, $5,500.00.

1906, Juanita, "Drink Coca-Cola Delicious Refreshing," framed, matted, under glass, 7" x 15", $4,000.00.

Calendars

"Drink Coca-Cola," brass perpetual desk, EX $150.00

1891, from ASA Chandler & Co. featuring girl in period dress holding sport racquet with full pad moved to reveal full face of sheet, rare, EX....$10,500.00

1904, Lillian Nordica standing by table with a glass, 7" x 15", EX......$4,000.00

1905, Lillian Nordica standing beside table holding fan, table has a glass, framed, matted, and under glass, 7" x 15", EX $4,500.00

1907, "Drink Coca-Cola Delicious Refreshing, Relieves Fatigue, Sold Everywhere 5¢" featuring woman in period dress holding up a glass of Coca-Cola, EX $5,500.00

1908, "Drink Coca-Cola Relieves Fatigue Sold Everywhere 5¢," top only, double this price if calendar is complete, 7 x 14, EX..$1,500.00

1911, the Coca-Cola Girl, "Drink Delicious Coca-Cola," framed under glass, 10" x 17", Hamilton King, M $3,200.00

1913, top, girl in white hat with red ribbon, value would double if complete, rare piece matted and framed under glass, EX, $3,000.00.

1917, Constance, with glass, full pad, framed and matted under glass, EX, $1,800.00.

1912, "Drink Coca-Cola Delicious and Refreshing," wrong calendar pad, correct pad should be at bottom of picture, King, EX ..$2,000.00

1914, Betty, with full pad and original metal strip at top, VG ..$1,000.00

1916, Elaine with glass, partial pad, under glass in frame, 13" x 32", M............................$1,500.00

1916, World War I Girl holding a glass, she also appears holding a bottle of another version, wrong pad, framed, 13" x 32", EX $1,500.00

1918, June Caprice with glass, framed under glass, G..........$350.00

1919, Knitting Girl, great art work of girl with bottle and a knitting bag, partial pad, framed under glass, 13" x 32", EX $2,200.00

1920, Garden Girl with a bottle, actually at a golf course, framed under glass, 12" x 32", M ..$1,700.00

1921, model sitting beside flowers with a glass, known as the Autumn Girl, partial pad, framed under glass, 12" x 32", M $1,300.00

1924, Smiling Girl in period dress holding a glass with a bottle close by, framed under glass, 12" x 24", Beware: Reproductions exist. M, $900.00.

1927, "The Drink that Makes The Whole World Kin," with bottle in oval frame at lower left, framed under glass, M, $900.00.

1922, girl at baseball game with a glass, framed under glass, 12" x 32", NM $1,800.00

1923, girl with shawl and a bottle with a straw, full pad, framed under glass, 12" x 24", VG $700.00

1925, girl at party with white fox fur and a glass, framed under glass, 12" x 24". Beware: Reproductions exist. M $900.00

1926, girl in tennis outfit holding a glass, with a bottle sitting by the tennis racquet, framed under glass, 10"x18", M $1,000.00

1928, model in evening wear holding glass, partial pad, framed under glass, 12" x 24", M $850.00

1927, "The Drink that Makes The Whole World Kin," with bottle in oval frame at lower left, framed under glass, M...$900.00

1929, girl in green dress, string of beads, glass and bottle, full pad, framed under glass, 12" x 24", M..........$950.00

1930, woman in swimming attire sitting on rock with canoe in foreground with bottles, display partial pad, framed under glass, 12" x 24", M $950.00

1933, the Village Blacksmith with full pad, framed and under glass, 12" x 24", Frederic Stanley, M, $750.00.

1936, 50th Anniversary, older man at small boat and a young girl enjoying a bottle, full pad, framed under glass, 12" x 24", N. C. Wyeth, M, $750.00.

1934, girl on porch playing music for elderly gentleman with cane, full pad, framed under glass, 12" x 24", Rockwell, M $700.00

1935, boy with a bottle sitting on a stump fishing, full pad, framed under glass, 12" x 24", Rockwell, Beware: Reproductions exist. M............$550.00

1937, boy walking, fishing pole over his shoulder, holding bottles, framed under glass, 12" x 24", M $525.00

1941, girl wearing ice skates sitting on log, displaying a bottle, full pad displays two months at same time, EX ..$375.00

1942, "America Love It or Leave It" from Brownsville, Tenn., featuring a drum & fife attachment, with monthly pads, EX $95.00

1943, pocket, "Tastes like Home," small, with all months shown on one front sheet, sailor drinking from a bottle, EX $35.00

1943, military nurse with a bottle, full pad displays two months at same time, EX $325.00

1945, girl in head scarf with snow falling in the background, full pad, EX $275.00

1946, Sprite Boy on cover with two months and a scene on each page, framed under glass, EX, $1,250.00.

1953, Boy Scout, Cub Scout, Explorer Scout in front of Liberty Bell, Coca-Cola Bottling Works, Greenwood, Mississippi, framed and matted under glass, Rockwell, EX, $350.00.

1948, girl in coat and gloves, holding a bottle, full pad, EX............$300.00

1952, "Coke adds Zest," party scene with a girl serving bottles from tray, full calendar pad, M $150.00

1953, "Work Better Refreshed," work scenes, woman in work scarf in center holding bottle, full pad, M $150.00

1954, "Me, too!" 1953 Santa cover sheet, full pad, owner recorded high and low temperatures of each day, VG ..$140.00

1954, reference edition with full pad featuring Santa with bottle, EX..$75.00

1956, "There's nothing like a Coke," full pad, featuring girl pulling on ice skates, M $135.00

1957, "The pause that refreshes," girl holding ski poles and bottle, EX..$80.00

1958, snow scene of a boy and girl with a bottle, "Sign of Good Taste," full pad, M $175.00

1960, "Be Really Refreshed," featuring man and woman holding skis, each with a bottle, full pad, M.....................$75.00

1960, reference with puppies in Christmas stockings, EX $20.00

1970, "It's the real thing," Coca-Cola presented its new image here, one that many collectors don't care to collect, so the demand for 1970 or newer calendars is not great...yet!, M, $20.00.

Perpetual desk showing day, month, and year, 1920, EX, $300.00.

Muddy River Trading Co./Gary Metz

Tin, calendar holder with daily tear sheets at bottom featuring tin button at top, red & white, 1950s, 8" x 19", EX, $400.00.

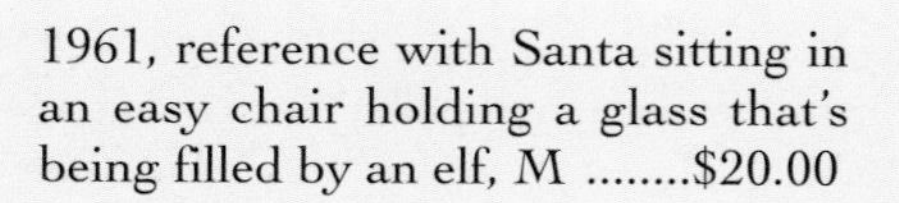

1961, reference with Santa sitting in an easy chair holding a glass that's being filled by an elf, M $20.00

1963, reference edition with Santa Claus in middle of electric train display in front of Christmas tree with helicopter flying around his head, holding a bottle, M $25.00

1964, reference featuring Santa standing by a fireplace with his list and a bottle, M $20.00

1965, reference edition with Santa and children, M $20.00

1964, "Things go better with Coke," featuring a woman reclining on a couch while a man is offering her a bottle, M $85.00

1967, reference edition with Santa Claus sitting at desk with a bottle, EX $12.00

1967, "For the taste you never get tired of," featuring five women with trophy, full pad, M $50.00

1968, "Coke has the taste you never get tired of," girl looking at 45rpm record and holding a bottle, with full pad, M $75.00

Change receiver, ceramic, with dark lettering and red line outline "The Ideal Brain Tonic, For Headache and Exhaustion," 1899, EX, $5,500.00.

Change, featuring the Coca-Cola Girl, 1910, King, EX, $550.00.

1969, reference edition showing Holiday Greetings, bottle on front, M $8.00

1970, reference edition featuring Santa with a bottle, M $10.00

1972, cloth featuring Lillian Nordica, EX $5.00

Tin, embossed calendar holder with a new 1988 pad, with "Drink" fishtail at top, red and white, 1960s, 9" x 13", G $125.00

Tin fishtail calendar holder with daily tear sheets at bottom, red & white, 1960s, 9" x 13", EX ..$150.00

Trays

Change, "Drink a Bottle of Carbonated Coca-Cola," 1903, 5½" dia, EX $5,000.00

Change, featuring the Coca-Cola Girl by Hamilton King, 1909 – 10, 4⅜" x 6⅛", King, VG $350.00

Change, featuring Hilda Clark, round, 1903, 6" dia, VG ..$2,300.00

Change receiver, glass, "Drink Coca-Cola 5¢," 1907, 7" dia, EX..$1,100.00

Serving, Betty, manufactured by Stelad Signs, Passaic, New Jersey, oval, 1914, 12½" x 15¼". Beware of reproductions. EX, $750.00.

Muddy River Trading Co./Gary Metz

Serving, "Coca-Cola" with good litho by Western Coca-Cola Bottling Company of Chicago, Illinois, without the sanction of the Coca-Cola Company, 1908, VG, $4,500.00.

Change receiver, Griselda Change, 1905, 13" x 13", EX $875.00

Change receiver, Hilda Clark, glass, 1900, 8½" dia, EX $4,000.00

Christmas serving tray, there are many variations of this tray, 1973, EX $10.00

Serving, Autumn Girl, this model isfeatured on the 1922 calendar, rectangular, 1920s, 10½" x 13¼", EX............$800.00

Serving, boy and dog, boy is holding sandwich and a bottle, 1931, 10½" x 13¼", Rockwell, EX $775.00

Serving, Captain James Cook bicentennial, produced to celebrate landing at Nootka Sound, B.C, "Coca-Cola" on back, 1978, EX $25.00

Serving, "Drink Coca-Cola Relieves Fatigue," oval, 1907, 10½" x 13¼", EX.......................................$2,250.00

Serving, Coca-Cola Girl holding a glass, 1913, 10½" x 13¼", King, Beware of reproductions. EX..$900.00

Serving, featuring Betty, rectangular, 1914, 10½" x 13¼", Beware of reproductions. EX................$775.00

Serving, featuring the famous Maureen O'Sullivan and Johnny Weismuller both holding a bottle, 1934, 13¼"x10½". Beware of reproductions. EX, $800.00.

Serving, "Drink Coca-Cola, Delicious and Refreshing," girl on dock, Sailor Girl, 1940, 13¼" x 10½", EX, $300.00.

Serving, featuring the Coca-Cola Girl, this was the first rectangular tray used by the Coca-Cola Company by American Art Works, Inc., 1909, 10½" x 13¼", King. Beware of reproductions. EX $1,100.00

Serving, featuring a couple receiving curb service, 1927, 13¼" x 10½", G $625.00

Serving, featuring Elaine, manufactured by Stelad Signs Passaic Metal Ware Company, Passaic, New Jersey, rectangular, 1916, 8½" x 19". Beware of reproductions. EX $575.00

Serving, featuring girl at party, 1921, 10½" x 13¼", EX $475.00

Serving, featuring girl on arm of chair in party dress, Hostess, 1936, 10½" x 13¼", EX $375.00

Serving, featuring girl on beach in chair with a bottle, 1932, 10½" x 13¼", EX............................$635.00

Serving, featuring girl running on beach with bottles in each hand, 1937. Beware of reproductions. EX..$300.00

Serving, featuring ice skater on log with bottle, 1941, 10½" x 13¼", EX ..$325.00

Serving, featuring a pull cart with a picnic basket, 1958, 13¼" x 10½", EX, $25.00.

Serving, featuring bird house full of flowers, French version, 1950s, 10½" x 13¼", EX, $110.00.

Serving, featuring Lillian Nordica on Canadian commemorative, 1968, 10½" x 13¼", EX $85.00

Serving, featuring movie star Madge Evans, manufactured by American Art Works, Inc., Coshocton, Ohio, 1935, 10½" x 13¼", EX $375.00

Serving, featuring red headed woman in yellow scarf with a bottle, 1950s, 10½" x 13¼". Beware of reproductions. EX................$100.00

Serving, featuring the movie star, Francis Dee, 1933, 10½" x 13¼", EX $425.00

Serving, featuring the Smiling Girl holding a glass, tray can have either a brown or maroon border, add $200.00 for maroon tray, 1924, 10½" x 13¼", EX $675.00

Serving, featuring the Summer Girl, manufactured by the H. D. Beach Company, Coshocton, Ohio, 1922, 10½" x 13¼", EX $825.00

Serving, Flapper Girl, 1923, 10½" x 13¼", EX.............................$400.00

Serving, Garden Girl, 1920, 13¼" x 16½", EX........................$875.00

Serving, Juanita, oval, "Drink Coca-Cola, In Bottles 5¢, at Fountains 5¢," 1906, 10½" x 13¼", EX, $2,500.00.

Serving, Menu Girl holding a bottle in her hand, 1950s, 10½" x 13¼", EX, $75.00.

Serving, girl in afternoon with a bottle, produced by American Art Works Inc., Coshocton, Ohio, 1938, 10½" x 13¼", EX $275.00

Serving, girl in swimsuit holding bottle, promoting bottle sales, 1929, 10½" x 13¼", VG $600.00

Serving, girl on a spring board, 1939, 10½" x 13¼", EX $300.00

Serving, "Hambly's Beverage Limited," featuring World War I girl, 60th anniversary, 1977, EX ..$15.00

Serving, "Here's a Coke for you," more than three versions of this tray, 1961, 13¼" x 10½", EX........................$20.00

Serving, promoting bottle sales, bobbed hair girl drinking from bottle with a straw, 1928, 10½"x13¼", EX....$650.00

Serving, promoting bottle sales, girl in red swim cap and bathing suit with a towel, 1930, EX........................$450.00

Serving, promoting fountain sales featuring girl in yellow swimsuit, produced by American Art Works Inc. of Coshocton, Ohio, 1929, 10½" x 13¼", EX $475.00

Victorian Girl, "Drink Coca-Cola, Refreshing, Delicious," woman drinking from a glass, 1897, 9¼" dia., EX, $14,000.00.

Serving, two women at car with bottles, because of metal needed in the war effort this was the last tray produced until after World War II, 1942, EX, $325.00.

Serving, promoting fountain sales, girl on phone, "meet me at the soda fountain," 1930, 10½" x 13¼", EX $425.00

Serving, promoting fountain sales with soda person (the term "soda jerk" wasn't used until much later), 1928, 10½"x13¼", EX $650.00

Serving, round, "Drink a Bottle of Carbonated Coca-Cola, The Most Refreshing Drink in the World," 1903, 9¾" dia, EX $6,500.00

Serving, St. Louis Fair, oval, 1909, 13½"x16½", EX $2,700.00

Serving, sports couple, 1926, 10½" x 13¼", Beware of reproductions. EX $725.00

Serving, with Garden Girl, 1920, 10½" x 13¼", EX $750.00

TV assortment, 1956, 18¾" x 13½", EX............................$15.00

TV, Duster Girl, 1972, 10¾" x 14¾", EX...............................$5.00

TV, Thanksgiving, 1961, 18¾" x 13¾", EX.............................$15.00

Booklet, The Coca-Cola Bottler, 1940, EX, $30.00.

Booklet, The Charm of Purity, 1920s, G, $35.00.

Advertisement from the *Chicago Daily News*, full page, 1908, EX, $10.00.

Muddy River Trading Co./Gary Metz

Paper Goods

Alphabet Book of Coca-Cola, 1928, EX..$65.00

Book cover, America is Strong... because America is Good! Dwight Eisenhower on front, 1950s, EX..$8.00

Book, 1942 advertising price list, 1942, EX $190.00

Book, 1943 advertising price list, 1943, EX $225.00

Book, 1944 advertising price list, 1944, EX $250.00

Book cover for school book, 1940 – 50s, white and red, EX $8.00

Book, *Illustrated Guide to the Collectibles of Coca-Cola*, Cecil Munsey, 1972, EX $85.00

Booklet, *Easy Hospitality*, 1951, EX $8.00

Booklet, *Know Your War Planes*, 1940s, EX $45.00

Booklet, *Profitable Soda Fountain Operation*, 1953, EX $65.00

Paper Goods

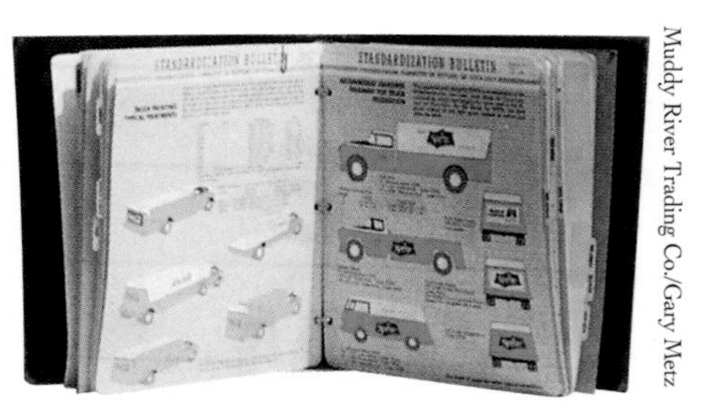

Muddy River Trading Co./Gary Metz

Bulletins book with Coca-Cola bulletins from the '50s and '60s featuring some great information, 1950s, G, $25.00.

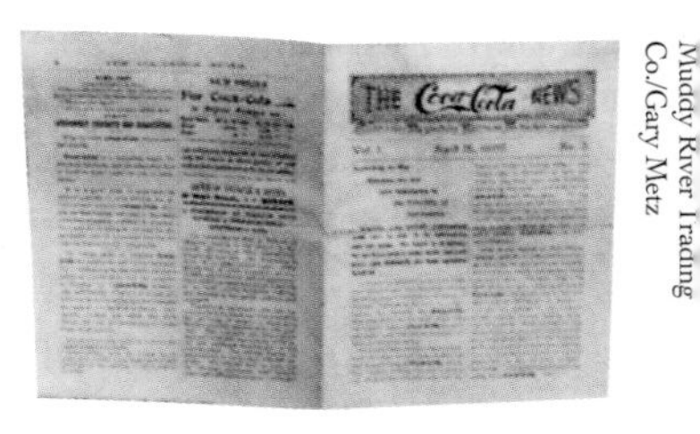
THE Coca-Cola NEWS

Muddy River Trading Co./Gary Metz

***Coca-Cola News*, 3rd edition, dated April 15, 1896, very hard to find, 1896, 6" x 8", NM, $125.00.**

Check, "Globe Bank & Trust Co., Paducah, Ky.," signed by Paducah Ky. bottler Luther Carson, 1908, EX, $100.00.

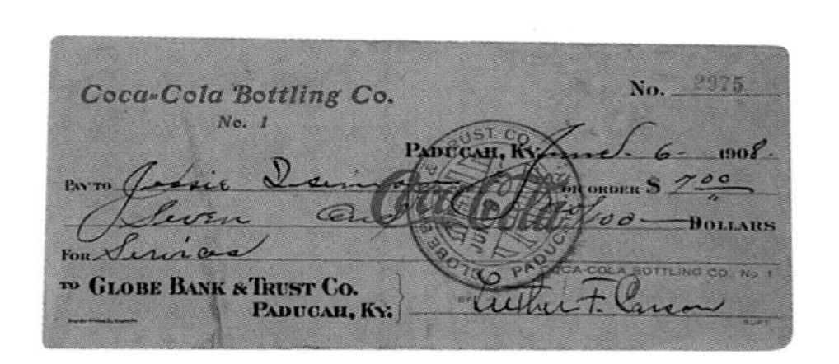
Coca-Cola Bottling Co. No. 2975
No. 1
Paducah, Ky. June 6 1908
Pay to ... or order $ 7.00
Seven and 00/100 Dollars
For Services
To Globe Bank & Trust Co. Paducah, Ky.
Luther F. Carson

Booklet, *The Romance of Coca-Cola*, 1916, EX $75.00

Bottlers' advertising price list, 1933, EX $190.00

Bottlers' advertising price list, 1935, EX $200.00

Bottlers' advertising price list, 50th Anniversary, 1936, EX $250.00

Bottlers' advertising price list, January 1932, 1932, EX $185.00

Bottlers' magazine, *The Red Barrel*, 1940, EX $15.00

Cap saver bag, for saving caps to redeem for cash from bottler at Bethlehem, Pa., red & white, 2½" x 5", EX $17.00

Comic book, "Refreshment Through The Ages," 1951, EX.............$25.00

Confederate souvenir bill, "Accept No Imitations," 1915, EX....$130.00

Convention packet, 14th Annual Coca-Cola Convention at Philadelphia, 1988, MIB $30.00

Coupon, featured 12 packs, 1950s, EX $8.00

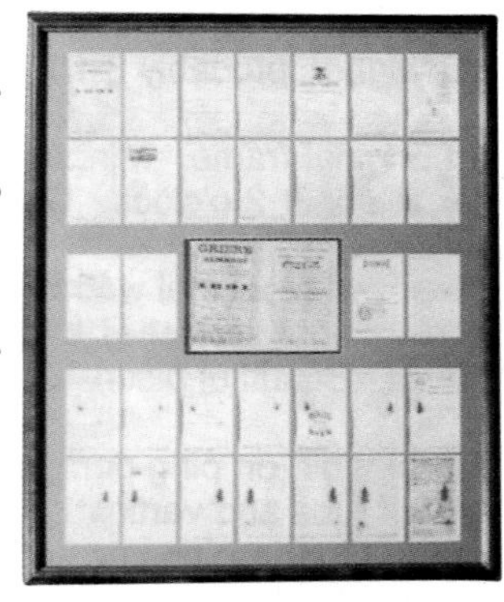

Muddy River Trading Co./Gary Metz

Grier's Almanac **featuring a large amount of advertising from Coca-Cola, and Asa Chandler, druggist, matted and framed, rare and hard to find, 1891, F, $1,300.00.**

Muddy River Trading Co./Gary Metz

Handbook used for sales preparation in retail stores, white lettering on red, 1950s, EX, $15.00.

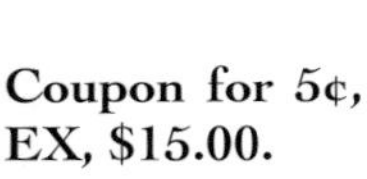

Coupon for 5¢, EX, $15.00.

Coupon, for free six pack with return of empty six pack featuring Santa Claus, issued from bottling company in Youngstown, Ohio, white lettering on light green background with Santa in 4-color, 6" x 3", EX $5.00

Coupon, for six free bottles of Coke with purchase of twelve pack, red and green on white, 6" x 3½", G....................................$5.00

Coupon, good for six pack of Coke when five are accumulated, red & green lettering on light green background, 3½" x 2", EX $5.00

Driver's license holder featuring bottle in hand from Terra Haute, Ind., dark blue lettering on light blue background, 2" x 3½", EX......$20.00

Halloween promotional package for dealers, 1954, EX $20.00

Health record, My Daily Reminder, Compliments of Sanford Coca-Cola Bottling Co, Sanford, N.C. Phone 20, 1930s, EX $12.00

Invitation to attend the opening of the Paducah, Ky., Coca-Cola plant, with picture of the bottling plant at top of sheet, 1939, G $25.00

Muddy River Trading Co./Gary Metz

Magazine ad featuring Lillian Nordica and a coupon at bottom, matted framed and under glass, 1904, EX, $110.00.

You Are Cordially Invited To The Opening

OF THE NEW HOME OF

Paducah Coca-Cola Bottling Co.

TUESDAY, JUNE TWENTIETH—Hours 1 to 5 and 7 to 9:30 P. M.

SPECIAL OPEN HOUSE FOR OUR COLORED CUSTOMERS AND FRIENDS WILL BE HELD WEDNESDAY, JUNE 21st ... EVERYONE IS INVITED

MUSIC • ENTERTAINMENT • COCA-COLA TO EACH VISITOR

NO CHILDREN ADMITTED UNLESS ACCOMPANIED BY ADULTS

PADUCAH COCA-COLA BOTTLING CO.

BROADWAY AND LA BELLE AVENUE — PADUCAH, KENTUCKY

Newspaper, *Paducah Sun-Democrat*, June 18, 1939, advertising the opening of a new bottling plant, F, $50.00.

Muddy River Trading Co./Gary Metz

Price list with great colors and period graphics in book form, 1941, EX, $325.00.

Letter, Asa G. Chandler, framed and matted, 1889, EX $175.00

Magazine ad featuring Lillian Nordica with the original coupon attached, 1904, 6½" x 9¾", EX $250.00

Magazine cover, front and back, *The Housewife*, June 1910, framed, The A. D. Poster Co, Publisher, New York, 1910, G $165.00

Menu sheet, "Today's Menu" featuring artwork of button and glass in lower page corners, green on white, 1950s, 6" x 11", EX $5.00

Menu sheet, "Today's Menu" featuring "goes good with food," artwork of glass in red banner at bottom, green on white, 1950s, 6" x 11", EX....$5.00

National Geographic Coca-Cola ads, full set, EX...........................$300.00

Notepad, pocket size, white lettering on red, 1943, 4" x 6", EX $15.00

Postcard from Charleston, Ill., good for free bottle of Coke, red lettering on white, 5" x 3", G $9.00

Route coupon from Paducah, Ky., EX $15.00

Score pads, "Spotter," "Drink Coca-Cola Delicious and Refreshing," and military nurse in uniform, 1940, EX, $10.00 each.

Muddy River Trading Co./Gary Metz

Sheet music "Nearer My God to Thee," in antique frame featuring artwork of Juanita, 1920s, 10½" x 13¼", G, $200.00.

Sheet music of "My Old Kentucky Home" featuring Juanita on cover with a glass, 1906, EX, $850.00.

Rand McNally Auto Road Map of Illinois with a Coca-Cola advertisement on the back cover, 1920s, G $35.00

Report card holder with 1923 bottle, 1930s, EX $85.00

Return ticket showing price of returned bottle deposit, G..........$10.00

Sack for popcorn from jungleland with "Drink Coca-Cola" logo in center featuring art work of tiger face, orange, red, black, 4" x 15", EX..............$12.00

School book cover with Sprite Boy, 1940 – 50s, EX $5.00

Score pad, American Women's Volunteer Service, 1940s, EX $15.00

Score pad for playing cards, six pack in spotlight "easy to serve, good with food," green on white, 4" x 11", EX $5.00

Service manual and parts catalog for VMC, manufactured Vendolator Mfg. Co. in leatherette book, 1950s, 8" x 9", EX $300.00

Sheet music, "It's the Real Thing," 1969, EX $10.00

Slide chart for figuring profits on sales of Coca-Cola, G............$10.00.

Cardboard foldout with Sprite Boy from the Coca-Cola bottler at Memphis, Tenn., 1951, F, $50.00.

Cardboard with rolled paper handle, "Drink Coca-Cola the Pause that Refreshes," 1930, $155.00.

Photos courtesy Muddy River Trading Co./Gary Metz

Wild flower study cards for schools, complete set consists of 20 cards and envelopes, 1920 – 30, VG ....$60.00 set

Writing tablet featuring Sprite Boy and safety ABC's, 1950s, EX $6.00

Writing tablet, Pure As Sunlight, 1930s, EX $20.00

Writing tablet, wildlife of the United States, 1970s, EX $5.00

Writing tablet, with Silhouette Girl, 1940s, EX $10.00

Fans

Bamboo with front and back graphics, "Keep Cool, Drink Coca-Cola," Oriental lady drinking a glass of Coca-Cola on opposite side, 1900, VG $150.00

Cardboard foldout from Atlanta Coca-Cola Bottling Company, EX......$50.00

Cardboard foldout from the Coca-Cola Bottling Co., Bethlehem, Pa., 1950s, EX $45.00

Cardboard on wooden handle, "Enjoy Coca-Cola," 1960s, EX $15.00

Cardboard with rolled paper handle, poem on cover, 1930s, EX, $135.00.

"And one for you," girl on blanket holding bottle," 1934, $85.00.

"Be Prepared, Be Refreshed," Boy Scout at cooler with a bottle in each hand, 1940s, M, $15.00.

Cardboard on wooden handle, with Sprite Boy, "Have A Coke," 1950s, EX $55.00

Cardboard with wooden handle, "Buy by the Carton, 6 for 25¢," Memphis, Tenn., 1930s, EX ..$60.00

Cardboard with wooden handle, "Drink Coca-Cola" with bottle in spotlight, 1930s, EX $75.00

Cardboard with wooden handle from the Coca-Cola Bottling Works of Greenwood, Miss., "Enjoy Coca-Cola," 1960s, EX $15.00

Blotters

"A pure drink of natural flavors," 1929, EX $150.00

Bottle in hand over the earth, 1958, EX $10.00

Bottle, large, "Over 60 million a Day," 1960, EX $8.00

Boy Scouts, "Wholesome Refreshment," 1942, EX $8.00

Coca-Cola being enjoyed by a policeman, 1938, EX..............$25.00

"Good with food. Try It," plate of food with two bottles, 1930s, M, $50.00.

Muddy River Trading Co./Gary Metz

Canadian blotter with ruler and protractor markings on edges, hard to find piece, 1930s, NM, $275.00.

Muddy River Trading Co./Gary Metz

"The Pause That Refreshes," 1930, EX, $40.00.

"Cold Refreshment," 1937, EX..$30.00

"Completely Refreshing," with disk upper left, 1942, EX $30.00

"Delicious and Refreshing," fountain service, 1915, EX..........$185.00

"Delicious, Refreshing," Sprite Boy and a bottle, 1951, EX $8.00

"Drink Coca-Cola," Atlanta, 1904, EX $400.00

"Drink...Delicious & Refreshing All Soda Fountain 5 cents," 1915, EX $175.00

"Friendliest drink on earth," a bottle in hand, 1956, 4"x8", EX........$10.00

Girl lying on her stomach, 1942, EX...$20.00

"The Greatest Pause On Earth," 1940, EX $75.00

"I Think It's Swell," 1944, 3½"x7½", EX $10.00

"The Pause That Refreshes," 1929, EX $85.00

"Pause that Refreshes" Coca-Cola blotter, 1941, NM $20.00

"So Refreshing, Keep on Ice," couple at ice box, 1927, M, $60.00.

Muddy River Trading Co./Gary Metz

The Coca-Cola Girl, 1910, NM, $775.00.

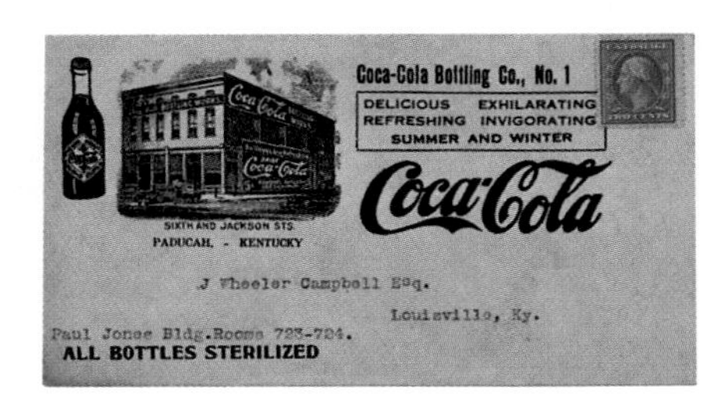

Coca-Cola Bottling Company, No. 1 at Paducah, Ky., with picture of bottling plant at Sixth and Jackson St., 1920s, EX, $35.00.

"Refresh Yourself," 1926, EX ..$35.00

"Restores Energy," 1906, red and white, EX..............................$130.00

Sprite Boy, 1947, EX $90.00

Sprite Boy with a bottle in the snow, 1953, G $8.00

"Thirst Knows No Season" blotter, 1947, NM $15.00

Three girls with bottles, disk at right, 1944, NM $30.00

50th Anniversary, 1936, EX ..$65.00

Postcards

Auto delivery truck with an even loaded bed and five men on board, 1913, EX $135.00

Bobby Allison & Coke, 1970s, NM $8.00

Bottling plant showing interior, 1905, EX $125.00

Duster girl, 1911, 3½"x5½", EX..$700.00

Exterior of a bottling plant showing the truck fleet in front of building, 1906, EX $150.00

International truck, 1940s, EX, $8.00.

Magazine, "Even the bubbles taste better," 1956, VG, $3.00.

The Housekeeper **cover, front and back, August 1909, framed, 1909, VG, $150.00.**

Folding, "Have You a Hobby?" showing a youngster on a rocking horse, 1910, EX....................$175.00

Free six bottles with wire handled carton commemorating 65th Anniversary, 1950s, EX $10.00

The Fulton Coca-Cola Bottling Co., 1909, EX $150.00

Horse-drawn delivery wagon, 1900, EX $125.00

Postcard featuring picture of DuQuoin, Illinois, bottling plant, NM $30.00

Race car of Bobby Allison, 1973, EX $8.00

Trifold, showing profits sitting on top of globe, 1913, EX $150.00

Ads

Delineator featuring a city scene, 1921, EX $8.00

Human Life, color, arrow encircling lady, 1910, NM $85.00

Human Life, color, "Come In" with arrow encircling soda fountain, 1909, NM $55.00

Magazine, Sprite Boy looking at Santa in front of opened refrigerator, 1948, EX, $25.00.

Magazine, Sprite Boy at soda fountain wearing soda fountain hat, 1949, G, $25.00.

Ladies' Home Journal, "Enjoy Thirst," girl, straw and bottle, 1923, EX....$8.00

Ladies' Home Journal, girl, background showing golfers, 1922, EX $15.00

Ladies' Home Journal, snow scene and skiers with flare glass in hand, 1922, EX $8.00

Ladies' Home Journal, "Thirst Knows No Season" with calendar girl, December, 1922, EX..............$20.00

Magazine, featuring Lillian Nordica and a Coke, matted and framed, 1904, NM $110.00

Magazine, "Scorching Hot Day," arrow above test, 1909, EX ..$35.00

Massengale, lady and maid, 1906, EX......................................$110.00

National Geographic, cover, back, "You Taste Its Quality," 1951, F $3.00

Saturday Evening Post featuring black background and water skier, EX..$8.00

Seated girl, 1915, 14" x 19", EX..$140.00

Woman's World, 1920, EX $35.00

Biedenharm Candy Company, Vicksburg, Miss., embossed block print, Hutchinson Bottle, 1894 – 02, aqua, EX, $350.00.

Biedenharm Candy Company, Vicksburg, Miss., embossed lettering, block print on crown top bottle, 1900s, aqua, EX, $200.00.

Bottles

American Airlines LE commemorative bottle, 8 oz., NM $150.00

Analyst-Portfolio Managers Meeting, limited edition of 408 bottles produced, 1996, M $225.00

Annie Oakley Days LE commemorative, 1985, NM....................$65.00

Atlanta Christian College, 1987, 10 oz., NM $8.00

Atlanta Falcons, NM $8.00

Baskin Robbins LR commemorative bottle, NM............................$150.00

Biedenharm Candy Company with applied paper label and "Coca-Cola" in script on bottle shoulder, 1905, aqua, EX $175.00

Biedenharm Candy Company, Vicksburg, Miss., with script "Coca-Cola" on base edge, all embossed, 1905, aqua, EX $130.00

Block print embossed on side in circle from Sedalia, Mo., 6½", aqua, EX $35.00

Carbonation tester used before the introduction of pre-mix, extremely hard to locate since normally only the bottlers had these items, EX, $500.00.

Muddy River Trading Co./Gary Metz

Ceramic syrup jug with paper label, tall, two-color stoneware, hardest to find, 1900s, 10" tall, VG, $2,600.00.

The Coca-Cola Bottling Company, six-sided body, 1920 – 30, aqua, EX, $50.00.

Block print embossed on base with fluted sides, 7 oz., clear, EX ..$40.00

Block print on shoulder, C.C.B. Company from Raton, N.M., embossed, 6 oz., aqua, EX $25.00

Cal Ripken Commemorative, 1996, M $4.00

California State Fair LE commemorative bottle, 1995, NM $5.00

Casey's General Store 25th anniversary LE commemorative bottle, 1968 – 93, NM $100.00

Casey's General Store 25th Anniversary 1968 – 1993, NM $135.00

Clemson, 1981, NM $5.00

Coca-Cola safe truck driving rodeo limited ed. commemorative, M $160.00

Commemorative Hutchinson style, "Coca-Cola 1894 – 1979," 1979, 7¼"h, M..................................$35.00

Commemorative reproduction of 1927 bottle used on luxury liners, green glass with green and red label, foil covered neck and top, 1994, M $65.00

Glass display 1923 Christmas bottle with display cap, 1930s, 20" tall, F, $250.00.

Double diamond, script "Coca-Cola" inside diamond from Toledo, Ohio, 1900 – 10s, 6 oz., amber, EX, $110.00.

Embossed script "Coca-Cola" at edge of base with unusual shoulder, clear, EX, $65.00.

Dallas Cowboys silver season commemorative, 1984, 10 oz., M $75.00

Dallas Cowboys Superbowl XXX commemorative, 8 oz., M $65.00

Domino's commemorative, M ..$75.00

Easter Seals commemorative, M..$28.00

England Royal Wedding, featuring Union Jack flag with screw-on cap, 7-29-81, 8 oz., M $75.00

Embossed 24 set, yellow wooden case with red lettering, 1920s, 24 bottle case, yellow, EX................$150.00

George C. Snyder D•A•Y commemorative, issued only to plant stockholders to honor founder of bottling plant in Charlotte, N.C., 1-30-96, 8 oz., M......$395.00

Georgia Tech 75th Anniversary, 1984, NM $12.00

Glass jug with diamond paper label, 1910, one gal., clear, EX $250.00

Glass jug with paper label, 1960s, one gal., clear, EX $15.00

Gold bottle of Bellingrath Gardens & Homes, Mobile, Ala., limited edition, NM $28.00

Gold, 50th Anniversary 1899 – 1949, Everett Pidgeon in bottle cradle, 1949, EX, $200.00.

Gold, 100th Anniversary, 1986, EX, $45.00.

Gold commemorative, 3-bottle set, from Atlanta, Ga., in display case, 1996, M $129.00

Guam Liberation Day............$10.00

Hardee's LE commemorative celebrating opening of the 3000th restaurant, 1988, NM $50.00

Hardee's 3 great years LE commemorative, 1982 – 85, 1985, NM$25.00

Hardee's 35th anniversary LE commemorative, NM.....................$75.00

Happy Holidays, 1994, NM....$3.00

Independent Grocers Alliance, 70th anniversary commemorative, only 960 produced, 1996, M........$110.00

Jacksonville Jaguars limited edition commemorative No. 1, M........$3.00

Jacksonville Jaguars limited edition commemorative No. 2, M........$3.00

Jacksonville Jaguars limited edition commemorative No. 3, M........$3.00

Jeff Gordon Winston Cup Champion, 1995, NM $3.00

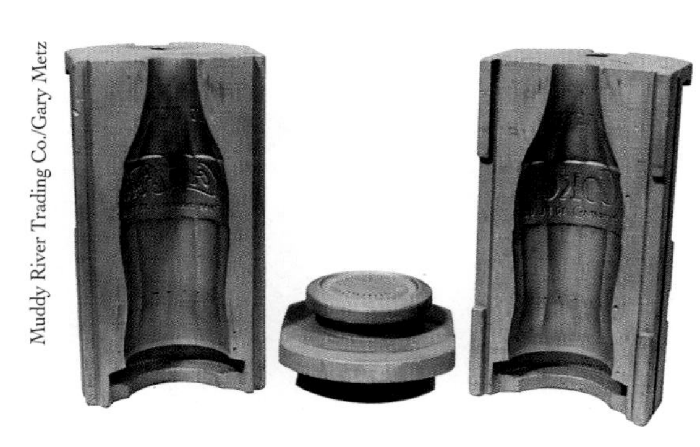

Muddy River Trading Co./Gary Metz

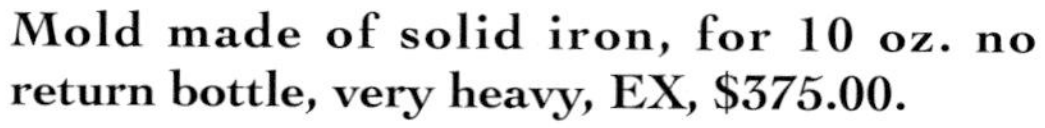

Mold made of solid iron, for 10 oz. no return bottle, very heavy, EX, $375.00.

National Convention, 75th Anniversary Hutchinson style bottle, fairly scarce, 1961, light aqua, EX, $200.00.

Kennesaw College National Softball Champs, 50 cases produced, M $14.00

Lamp with embossed "Coca-Cola" base, 1970s, 20", EX.......... $6,000.00

Long John Silver's LE commemorative, 8 oz., NM........................ $95.00

Mardi Gras, 1996, NM............ $3.00

McDonald's 40th partners, M.. $120.00

McDonald's Hawaii I, M $50.00

McDonald's Hawaii II, M $50.00

Mexican Christmas commemorative, 1993, M $26.00

Mexican Christmas commemorative, 1994, EX $21.00

Mexican Christmas bottle, 1996, M $22.00

Mickey Mouse Hawaii Toontown limited edition commemorative, given away with $200 grocery purchase in Hawaii between May and July 1994, M.......................... $10.00

Nahunta Fire Dept LE commemorative, M $80.00

Original paper label with script "Coca-Cola Beverage," reproduction labels are available, 1900 – 10, aqua, F, $100.00.

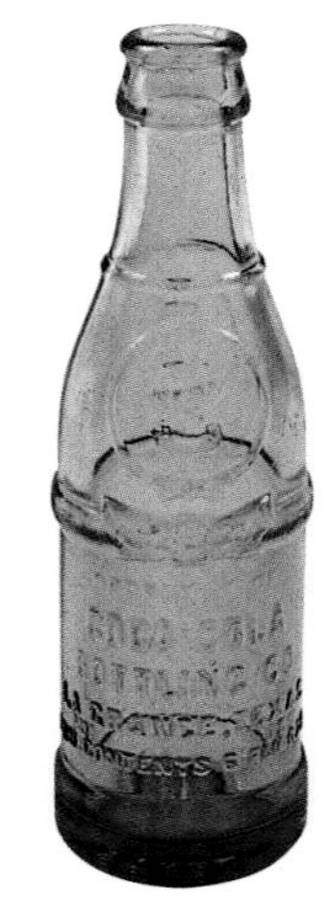

"Property of Coca-Cola Bottling Co, La Grange, Texas," in block print on body with embossed ribbon on shoulder, 6 oz., aqua, EX, $30.00.

Premix, 1920s, green, EX, $55.00.

Oklahoma Anniversary, regular capped, gold dipped with white lettering, dated 1903 – 67 on reverse, only 1,000 made make this a fairly scarce item, 1967, 6½ oz., gold, EX....$100.00

Olympic City commemorative, Atlanta Ga., 1996, 8 oz., M....$15.00

Pete Rose limited edition commemorative, M $95.00

Phoenix Coyotes hockey LE commemorative bottle with picture of moon, new, M $3.00

Pharmor, NM $275.00

Republican National Convention LE commemorative, 1996, M........$30.00

Ron Carew LE commemorative, NM $25.00

Ronald McDonald House charity commemorative, 1996, M $105.00

Root commemorative in box with silver clasp, 1971, aqua, EX $350.00

San Diego Padres, 1993, NM....$3.00

Script "Coca-Cola" in shoulder from Verner Springs Water Co, Greenville, S.C., 9", aqua, EX $55.00

Script "Coca-Cola" inside arrow circle, Louisville, Ky., 1910s, 6 oz., amber, EX, $75.00.

Seltzer, clear, from Coca-Cola Bottling Co., Cairo, Illinois, with applied color labeling featuring Ritz boy with tray, EX, $225.00.

Muddy River Trading Co./Gary Metz

Syrup bottle with wreath logo, with original jigger cap, nice heavy transfer onto bottle, 1910, NM, $700.00.

Script "Coca-Cola" on shoulder and Biedenharm in script on base, all lettering is embossed, 1900s, aqua, F..........$135.00

Seltzer, Coca-Cola Bottling Co., Morgantown, W.Va., clear with red lettering, VG $150.00

Seltzer, Fargo, North Dakota, EX $200.00

Seltzer, green fluted with gold etching, VG $200.00

Southwest Airlines commemorative featuring artwork of wings on bottle, 8 oz., M $125.00

Small tray bottle for toy cooler, 1951, 3½" tall, EX..................$15.00

St. Louis Rams, NM................$3.00

Standard top, "Coca-Cola" in block print from Mt. Vernon, Ill., embossed at base, 6 oz., aqua, EX...................$10.00

Straight-sided amber marked "Made at Williamstown, New Jersey," and "Made by Williamstown Glass Company," made by a mold, very rare, 1905 – 10, 3¼" tall, EX........$3,200.00

Styrofoam display, 1961, 42" tall, VG.....................................$210.00

Syrup can with paper label, featuring art work of glass 1940s, one gallon, NM, $525.00.

Syrup can with paper label, red & white, 1940s, one gallon, EX, $275.00.

Syrup keg with paper label on end, 1930s, 5-gallon, F, $100.00.

Photos courtesy Muddy River Trading Co./Gary Metz

Syrup, with applied label and original cap, EX........................$1,000.00

Test for 16 oz., "QC" on bottom for quality control, original sticker, scarce due to unusual size, 1940 – 60s, 16 oz., NM.....................$85.00

Ty Cobb commemorative, birthplace Banks County, 8 oz., NM......$75.00

Ty Cobb LE commemorative five-piece: The Georgia Peach; Royston Lodge Remembers; First in the Hall of Fame; The Boy, the Man, the Legend; Birthplace, Banks County, NM...................................$1,375.00

Tyber Island Centennial limited edition commemorative, 10 oz., M..$8.00

Wal-Mart Christmas, 1994, NM..$3.00

White Castle 75th anniversary LE commemorative bottle, NM ..$85.00

World of Coca-Cola 5th anniversary limited edition commemorative, 8 oz., M.......................................$6.00

York Rite Masonry, NM $20.00

Young Presidents commemorative, M $55.00

Muddy River Trading Co./Gary Metz

Anniversary glass given to John W. Boucher, 1936, NM, $375.00.

Muddy River Trading Co./Gary Metz

Flare 5¢ acid etched glass, 1912, EX, $875.00.

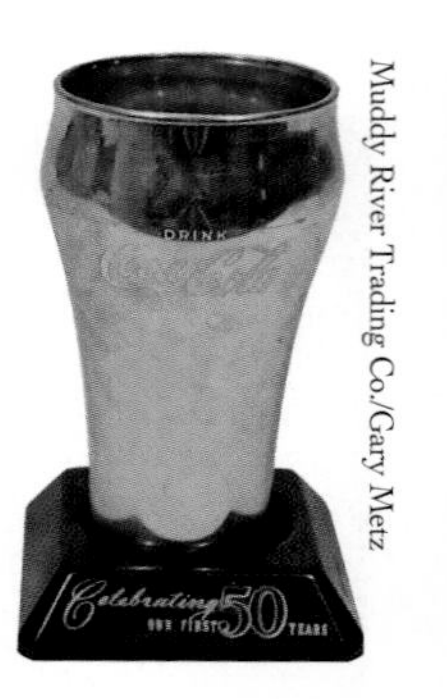

Muddy River Trading Co./Gary Metz

50th Anniversary, gold-dipped with plastic stand, 1950s, EX, $250.00.

Bell, with "Enjoy," set of four different sizes, EX, $12.00.

75th Anniversary, Paducah Coca-Cola Bottling Company, Inc., 1978, 10 oz., clear, EX $15.00

75th Anniversary, Thomas Bottling Company, 1974, amber, EX ..$75.00

Glasses

Bell, "Enjoy Coca-Cola," 1970s, EX ..$3.00

Bell with trademark in tail of C, 1930 – 40s, EX $40.00

Coca-Cola Holly Hobbie Christmas glass, 1980, EX $6.00

Flare, "Bottle Coca-Cola," 1916, EX $550.00

Flare, 50th anniversary, gold lettering from Somersworth, N.H., gold metallic on clear glass, 1966, 6 oz., EX $50.00

Flare, modified, "Coca-Cola," 1926, EX $125.00

Flare with syrup line, "Drink Coca-Cola," 1910s, EX..................$400.00

Flare, syrup line, 1900s, EX....$435.00

Muddy River Trading Co./Gary Metz

Creamer, "Drink Coca-Cola," 1930s, VG, $300.00.

Muddy River Trading Co./Gary Metz

Silver glass holder, beware of reproductions, 1900s, NM, $2,100.00.

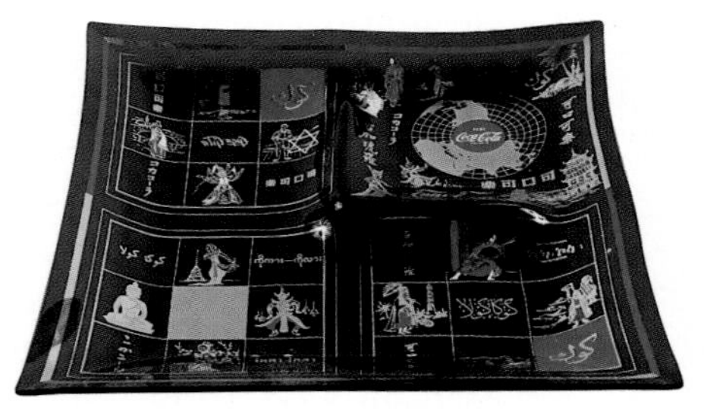

Dish, square, "Coca-Cola" world, 1960s, 11½" x 11½", EX, $125.00.

Fountain glass "Drink Fanta" clear glass, white lettering, 8 oz., EX..$10.00

Fountain glass, "Drink Tab" white lettering on clear glass, 8 oz., EX $10.00

Hour-glass "Enjoy Tab," yellow lettering on clear glass, EX..........$6.00

Pittsburg Steelers Hall of Fame/Coca-Cola, set of four, M $30.00

Soap box derby Coca-Cola glass from Akron, Ohio, hard to find, EX......................................$135.00

China

Dish, round, world, 1967, 7", EX..................................$100.00

Display bottle with original tin lid, 1923 bottle, 20", EX $260.00

Pitcher, red lettered "Coca-Cola" on glass, M $55.00

Plate, Swedish, 1969, 8¼" x 6¼", EX $100.00

Sandwich plate featuring bottle and glass in center, "Refresh Yourself," 1930s, 8¼" dia, G $775.00

Sandwich plate, "Drink Coca-Cola Refresh yourself," 1930s, 8¼", NM, $1,200.00.

Sandwich plate, "Drink Coca-Cola Refresh Yourself," Knowles China Co., 1931, NM, $375.00.

"Drink Coca-Cola Good with food," Wellsville China Co., 1940 – 50s, 7½", VG, $750.00.

Photos courtesy Muddy River Trading Co./Gary Metz

Sugar bowl complete with lid, "Drink Coca-Cola," 1930, M $350.00

Art Plates

Western Coca-Cola™ Bottling Co., featuring brunette, red hair scarf, holding pink rose, 1908 – 12, EX $350.00

Western Coca-Cola™ Bottling Co., featuring dark haired woman at angle to plate, 1908, 10" dia., EX $350.00

Western Coca-Cola™ Bottling Co., featuring dark haired woman, low drape across shoulders, 1908, 10" dia., EX....$350.00

Western Coca-Cola™ Bottling Co., featuring dark haired woman with yellow head piece, 1908 – 12, 10" dia, EX..................................$350.00

Western Coca-Cola™ Bottling Co., featuring long haired woman, body forward with head and eyes to the left, wearing a white drape off the shoulders, 1908 – 12, EX $450.00

Western Coca-Cola™ Bottling Co., featuring woman with auburn colored hair with a red adornment on the right side of her head, 1908, 10" dia., EX $350.00

Western Coca-Cola™ Bottling Co., if any art plate is in its original shadow box frame value can be doubled, 1908 – 12, EX, $500.00.

Celluloid and metal pocket mirror with the Hamilton King Coca-Cola girl on the front, 1911, 1¾" x 2¾", F, $150.00.

Celluloid and metal pocket mirror featuring Elaine, 1916, 1¾" x 2¾", G, $190.00.

Western Coca-Cola™ Bottling Co., featuring woman with long red hair and off the shoulder apparel, 1908–12, 10" dia, EX $300.00

Western Coca-Cola™ Bottling Co., profile of dark haired woman with a red head piece and a yellow blouse, 1908 – 12, 10", EX $350.00

Mirrors

Celluloid and metal, the Coca-Cola Girl, 1910, 1¾" x 2¾", Hamilton King, NM $550.00

Celluloid and metal, "Drink Coca-Cola," Elaine, 1916, 1¾" x 2¾", NM....................................$550.00

Celluloid and metal, "Drink Coca-Cola 5¢," 1914, 1¾" x 2¾", NM $600.00

Celluloid and metal, "Drink Delicious Coca-Cola" with the Coca-Cola girl, 1911, 1¾" x 2¾", Hamilton King, NM. Beware: Reproductions exist $550.00

Celluloid and metal pocket mirror featuring "Juanita," 1906, 1¾" x 2¾", F $85.00

Pocket mirror featuring the Coca-Cola girl, 1910, 1¾" x 2¾", EX, $250.00.

Glass, Silhouette Girl, with thermometer, 1939, 10"x14¼", VG, $850.00.

Mirror with thermometer "Drink Coca-Cola in Bottles," 1930s, 10" x 14", G, $325.00.

Glass front dial type thermometer "things go better with Coke" at top and "Drink" button at bottom, red lettering on white background, 1964, 12" round, EX, $300.00.

Photos courtesy Muddy River Trading Co./Gary Metz

Celluloid and metal, "Relieves Fatigue," 1907, 1¾" x 1¾", EX..................$600.00

Commemorative wall mirror featuring Hilda Clark produced for the 75th anniversary of the Chicago Coca-Cola Bottling Co., 1976, 28½" x 41", NM $425.00

Pocket, folding cardboard cat's head, "Drink Coca-Cola in bottles" on inside cover, 1920, EX ..$750.00

Pocket, "Wherever you go you will find Coca-Cola at all fountains 5¢," 1900s, G...............................$900.00

Thermometers

Cardboard pre-mix counter unit thermometer with mercury scale on left, comparison chart of thermometer reading to regulator setting on right, 1960s, VG $55.00

"Drink Coca-Cola in Bottles," Coca-Cola Bottling Co., Madisonville, Ky., 1920 – 1930s, 8" x 17½", EX $500.00

Glass front, "Drink Coca-Cola in Bottles" round needle type thermometer, white on red background, 1950s, 12", EX......................$170.00

Leather desk thermometer, 1930s, EX, $1,200.00.

Metal embossed Spanish bottle thermometer, 1950s, 6" x 18", EX, $150.00.

Metal die cut bottle thermometer, 1956, 5" x 17", NM, $160.00.

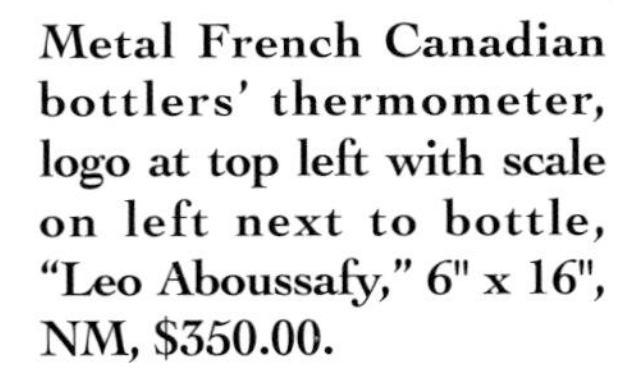

Metal French Canadian bottlers' thermometer, logo at top left with scale on left next to bottle, "Leo Aboussafy," 6" x 16", NM, $350.00.

Photos courtesy Muddy River Trading Co./Gary Metz

Liquid crystal readout showing temperature in both Celsius and Fahrenheit, scarce, 1970s, 10¼" sq, NM $120.00

Masonite, "Thirst knows no season" with angled thermometer scale, 1944, 7" x 17", NM $400.00

Metal bottle, 1953, 17" tall, EX..$90.00

Metal "cigar" thermometer, red & white, 1950s, 30" tall, F........$130.00

Metal framed mirror with thermometer on left side and Silhouette Girl across bottom, 1930s, EX $450.00

Metal gold Christmas bottle on oval base, gold on red, 1938, 7" x 16", EX $210.00

Metal, gold version double bottle, "Drink Coca-Cola," metal composition, 1942, 7" x 16", EX........$350.00

Metal and plastic, 12" Pam style with bottle outline in center on red background, outside circle is in green with black numbers, 1950s, EX $425.00

Metal thermometer with wooden back "Drink Coca-Cola, Coke Refreshes," 1950s, 8" x 36", M $3,300.00

Round glass front, "Enjoy Coca-Cola" dial type thermometer, white lettering on red background, 1960s, 12" round, EX, $170.00.

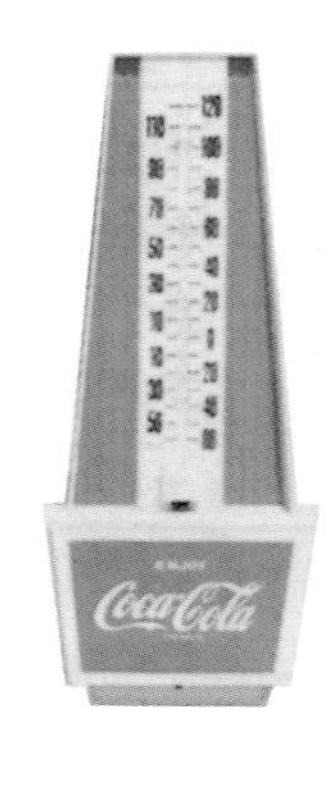

Plastic vertical scale thermometer, red and white, 1960s, 7" x 18", EX, $30.00.

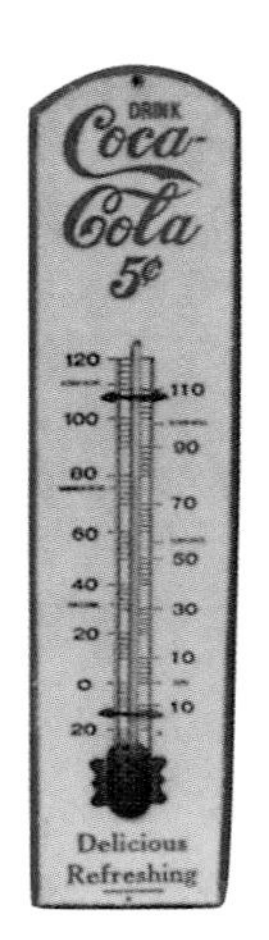

Wooden, "Coca-Cola 5¢" good graphics, red on white, 1905, 5" x 21", G, $400.00.

Photos courtesy Muddy River Trading Co./Gary Metz

Metal, stand-up, calculated in Celsius and Fahrenheit, 1940s, VG $15.00

Plastic and metal, round, "Drink Coca-Cola," fishtail with green on white, 1960s, NM $375.00

Porcelain, Canadian, Silhouette Girl, with red and yellow background, 1942, VG $400.00

Tin, die cut bottle, embossed, 1933, G $110.00

Tin, double bottle thermometer, 1941, 16" tall, NM...............$475.00

Tin, "Drink Coca-Cola in Bottles" Phone 612, Dyersburg, Tenn., with reminder notations for oil, grease, and battery, 1940s, VG $25.00

Tin, Silhouette Girl thermometer, "Drink Coca-Cola Delicious and Refreshing," 1930s, 6½" x 16", G $300.00

Carriers

Aluminum six pack carrier with separated bottle compartments, "Coca-Cola" is embossed on side, 1940 – 50s, EX $85.00

Bent wood with rounded corners and flat wood handle, 1940s, VG, $100.00.

Muddy River Trading Co./Gary Metz

Cardboard six pack carrier, 6 for 25¢, red and white, 1939, EX, $45.00.

Muddy River Trading Co./Gary Metz

Cardboard carton display, "Take enough home today," 1950s, 14" x 20" x 38", EX, $210.00.

Aluminum six pack carrier with wood and wire handle, red lettered "Drink Coca-Cola," 1950s, EX $75.00

Aluminum six pack king size carrier with wire handle, red lettered "Drink Coca-Cola" and "King Size," 1950, EX $75.00

Aluminum six pack with wire handle, separated bottle compartments, "Delicious Refreshing Coca-Cola" in white on red center panel, 1950s, EX $45.00

Cardboard, car window holder, 1950s, red and white, EX $25.00

Cardboard display rack, "Drink Coca-Cola Take Home a Carton," 1930s, VG $725.00

Cardboard, red and white, will hold four Family Size bottles, NOS, 1958, NM $6.00

Cardboard, six pack "Money back bottles return for deposit," dynamic wave logo, red and white, NOS, 1970s, EX $4.00

Cardboard, six pack, "Serve Ice Cold," 1930s, EX....................$85.00

Metal grocery cart two bottle holder with sign on front "Enjoy Coca-Cola while you shop, Place Bottles Here," 1950s, EX, $35.00.

Metal twelve pack, red lettering on yellow body, 1920–30s, G, $300.00.

Cardboard, twelve bottles, "Coca-Cola" in script, white on red, NOS, 1951, EX $15.00

Cardboard, waxed "In six Bottle cartons" with "Coca-Cola" button at left, will hold four six pack cartons, NOS, 1940s, M $45.00

Cardboard, white lettering on red, "Chill...Serve..." banner at top by cut-out carry handle, twelve bottles, NOS, 1950s, EX $15.00

Cardboard, white top with red lettering, red button, twelve bottles, NOS, 1960s, NM $5.00

Cardboard with metal handles, "Drink Coca-Cola" on front, "Have a Coke," "Picnic Cooler" on sides, red with white lettering, 1956, EX $130.00

48 bottle wooden shipping crate, 1910s, 9" x 18" x 25", VG $350.00

Masonite six pack carrier, 1940s, EX $65.00

Metal for car window, 1940s, white and red, EX $75.00

Metal three case bottle rack with "Place Empties Here, Thank You" sign at top, red, G $125.00

Muddy River Trading Co./Gary Metz

Salesman sample bulk case storage rack complete with plastic cases with bottles and castors, in original box, hard to find item, 1960s, 6" x 12" x 13", NM, $4,500.00.

Wooden with dovetail corner joints, "Refresh yourself Drink Coca-Cola in Bottles," black lettering, 1920s, VG, $250.00.

Muddy River Trading Co./Gary Metz

Wooden six pack carrier with bottle separators, "Pause...Go Refreshed" white on red, 1930s, EX, $450.00.

Metal vendor's carrier, red with white lettering; embossed on ends, front metal loop handle, 1950s, red, VG......$200.00

Metal and wire Canadian carrier and vendor for 18 bottles "Drink Coca-Cola Iced" on side panels, 1930s, 18 bottle, G $275.00

Metal and wire 18 bottle, Canadian, 1930 – 40, red, VG $275.00

Six pack carton wrapper, July 4th, 1930s, red, white, blue, EX......$350.00

Twelve bottle aluminum carrier with red panel on side, 1950s, EX $85.00

Wooden, "Drink Coca-Cola in Bottles," cut-out carrying handle, wings at end, 1940s, yellow, EX $95.00

Wooden, six pack, with end wings and bottle separators, white logo on red background, 1930 – 1940s, EX....................................$450.00

Wooden six pack with wood and wire handle, wings on side of carrier, 1930 – 40s, yellow, EX......$95.00

Wooden six pack with wooden handle featuring a cut-out hand hold, 1940s, EX $150.00

Muddy River Trading Co./Gary Metz

Floor cooler with base in form of picnic cooler, 1950s, 17" x 12" x 39", EX, $3,100.00.

Cooler, lift top fiberglass, built to resemble a Vendo V-81 vending machine, new, EX, $285.00.

Vending Machines

Cavalier Coca-Cola vending machine, model 96, vends 96 bottles and pre-cools 17 bottles, 1950s, EX $750.00

Glascock junior size cooler complete with cap catcher, 1929, EX ..$1,400.00

Jacobs vending machine model #26, upright shaped like a mailbox, very sought after but also the most common of Jacobs machines, 1940 – 50s, red, EX $1,100.00

Vendo coin changer with keys, reproduction sign, EX..........$625.00

Vendo model 39, a top entry drum type box with the coin mechanism on top, vends 39 bottles and pre-cools 42 bottles, not highly sought after in the past, but a nice machine whose value will increase, white lettering on red, 1940s, 34½"w x 34"h x 27½"d, EX $775.00

Vendo model 56, similar to the model 81, but without fluorescent tube in door, and the door on most versions has to be opened to observe selection, red & white, 1950s, 25"w x 52"h x 18¾"d, F $500.00

Mike and Debbie Summers

Vendo V-81, much sought after for home use due to its compact design and ability to dispense different size bottles, 1950s, 27" x 58" x 16", white on red, VG, $500.00.

Victor C-45A salesman's sample chest cooler, cardboard, 1940 – 1950s, G, $100.00.

Vendo model 83 vending machine, not in heavy demand due in large part to the fact they are so heavy, red & white, 1940s, 32½"w x 63"h x 18" d, EX $175.00

Vendo 39 vending machine, chest type with top drum and coin entry box, 1940s, 34½"w x 34"h x 27¼"d, F..$200.00

Vendo 44 Coca-Cola vending machine, unrestored in original condition, this is the jewel for collectors and is very sought after, vends 44 bottles and pre-cools 9 bottles, red and white, 1950s, 16"w x 57½"h x 15½"d, EX..$1,600.00

Vendo 81 Coca-Cola vending machine, one of the most sought after machines due in part to its compact design, original unrestored, red & white, 1950s, 27"w x 58"h x 16"d, F $450.00

Vendo V-23, box cooler that will vend 23 bottles, made in both a standard and deluxe version, fairly easy to find, 1940 – 50s, red and silver, EX $400.00

Vendo V-56, upright, will dispense 56 bottles, 1950s, red and white, EX....................................$700.00

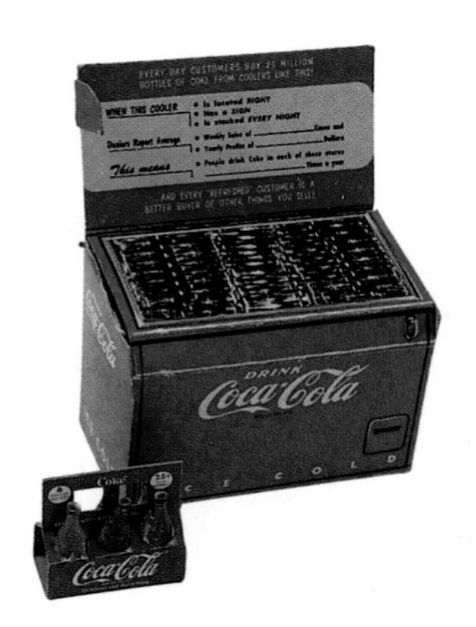

Westinghouse WE-6, salesman's sample, 1940 – 1950s, 4⅜" x 4" x 3", G, $100.00.

Muddy River Trading Co./Gary Metz

Zinc lined wet box for cooling and dispensing, "Help Yourself Drink Coca-Cola Deposit in Box 5¢," wood exterior, 1920s, F, $310.00.

Vendo V-81, dispenses 81 bottles, upright, this machine also sought after by collectors but is still fairly easy to find, 1950s, red and white, EX..$900.00

Vendo V-83, dispenses 83 bottles, very common, 1940–50, red, EX $200.00

Vendolator 27, known as the table top, this machine would set on a desk or special stand, dispenses 27 bottles, still fairly easy to find, 1940s, 24" x 27" x 19", red, EX $850.00

Westinghouse Master electric chest cooler, dispenses 144 bottles, fairly common, 1930 – 40, red, EX ..$300.00

Westinghouse model 42, embossed "Here's A Coke For You" on sides, early models were solid red, red & white, 1950s, 25"w x 53½"h x 20"d, EX $600.00

Westinghouse model 96, vends 96 bottles and will dispense both regular and King Size bottles, 1950s, 25"w x 75"h x 19½"d, F $550.00

Westinghouse salesman's sample, featuring open front, white on red, F ..$900.00

Westinghouse 3 Case Junior, ice cooled chest box, 1940 – 50s, red, EX $425.00

Airline Coca-Cola cooler with stainless steel cooler, white lettering on red, 1950s, G, $300.00.

Ball park vendor complete with canvas straps and opener, has divider and is insulated, 1940s – 50s, VG, $200.00.

Junior stainless steel cooler, 1950s, 12" x 9" x 14", EX, $650.00.

Photos courtesy Muddy River Trading Co./Gary Metz

Coolers

Airline style painted cooler with stainless liner, with opener on end, white lettering on red, 1950s, NM $375.00

Aluminum, 12 pack, 1950s, 12 pack, EX $85.00

Dispenser, refills from top, red metal with cream lettering, 1950s, VG $325.00

Insulated stadium vendor, no strap or opener, red, 1930s, F $250.00

Floor chest, embossed lettering, yellow and white lettering on red background with bottle at left side, 29" x 32½"h x 22"d, VG $950.00

Metal picnic, small, "Drink Coca-Cola in Bottles," 1950s, VG ..$130.00

Metal picnic, with bottle in hand decal, 1940 – 50s, 13" x 12" x 8", EX..$110.00

Metal, Progress Refrigerator Company, Louisville, Ky., featuring "Things go better..." logo embossed on front. With lift top lid, metal handles with opener under handle, white lettering on red background, F $100.00

Picnic cooler with original hand in bottle decals on each side, with bail handle, red, 1940s, 8" x 12" x 13", F, $100.00.

Muddy River Trading Co./Gary Metz

Salesman's sample, sale aid shaped like box cooler, EX, $85.00.

Muddy River Trading Co./Gary Metz

Stainless steel picnic cooler "Drink Coca-Cola" on front in red, 1950s, 6-pack, EX, $425.00.

Muddy River Trading Co./Gary Metz

Wooden cooler for iced bottles, with the original zinc lined tub, red on yellow, 1920s, 38" x 20" x 35", F, $950.00.

Plastic covered metal, by Royal Mieco Inc. Clinton, Okla., metal handles featuring "Drink" opener on side, white on red, P $75.00

Stadium vendor, "Have a Coke," 16" x 10" x 21", G..........................$50.00

Vinyl cooler bag featuring "drink" fishtail on front, red & white..1960s, 1" x 10" x 6", Riverside, G $85.00

Vinyl picnic with fishtail logo, shaped like a box with a fold-over top and strap, "Refreshing New Feeling," NM..........................$45.00

Radios

Bottle shaped, 1933, VG ..$3,300.00

Bottle shaped, AM/FM, plastic, 1970s, EX $35.00

Can with the dynamic wave, 1970s, EX $45.00

Cooler design, upright, J. Russell, 1970s, EX $110.00

Cooler, upright, 1950s, F $200.00

Cooler design, upright, 1960s, G $165.00

Muddy River Trading Co./Gary Metz

Cooler, prices on these vary greatly, some will go into the thousands, while others fall below the book price, remember condition, 1950s, red, VG, $625.00.

Muddy River Trading Co./Gary Metz

Cooler shaped crystal with ear piece, if all parts including instructions are present increase price to $200.00, EX, $175.00.

Extremely rare and hard to find, radio designed to resemble an airline cooler, top lifts to reveal controls, red & white, 1950s, G, $3,800.00.

Cooler design, upright, 1980s, EX $75.00

Cooler design, upright, with dynamic wave, 1970s, EX $125.00

Cooler, lights up and plays, 1950s, EX $900.00

Clocks

Anniversary style dome, 1950s, 3" x 5", EX $750.00

Boudoir, leather with gold logo at bottom, "Drink Coca-Cola So Easily Served," 1910, 3" x 8", G ..$1,300.00

Celluloid desk, Hilda Clark seated at table holding a glass in a holder, clock is in lower left portion of piece, working, rare and hard to find, 1901, 5½" x 7¾", EX....................$8,500.00

Counter, "Drink Coca-Cola Please Pay When Served," yellow numbers on black background, 19¼" x 9", VG $400.00

Desk, leather composition with "Drink Coca-Cola in Bottles 5¢" at top center over clock works and smaller bottles at lower right and left hand corners, 1910, 4⅓" x 6", EX $1,100.00

Muddy River Trading Co./Gary Metz

"Drink Coca-Cola in Bottles," wooden frame, 1939 – 40, 16" x 16", G, $175.00.

"Drink Coca-Cola 5¢ Delicious, Refreshing 5¢," Baird Clock Co., 15 day movement, working, 1896 – 99, EX, $6,500.00.

Muddy River Trading Co./Gary Metz

Light-up clock made by Modern Clock Advertising Company in Brooklyn, N.Y., aluminum case with solid plastic face that lights up, 1950s, 24" dia., EX, $550.00.

"Drink Coca-Cola" red and white plastic, round, EX $450.00

Gilbert case, "Drink Coca-Cola" in red lettering on clock face and decal of girl with a bottle on bottom glass door, 1910, 18" x 40", EX..$4,500.00

Gilbert key wound case, "Drink Coca-Cola" in red lettering on white clock face, "In Bottles 5¢" on pendulum door glass, 1916 – 20s. Beware: Reproductions exist. EX $1,300.00

Gilbert pendulum with original finish, 1930s, VG $1,200.00

Gilbert regulator with Gibson girl decal on glass, 1910, EX ..$6,000.00

Ingraham with restored regulator on bottom glass, some fade in to clock face, 1905, VG......................$950.00

Light-up advertising by Modern Clock Advertising Company in Brooklyn, N.Y., aluminum case, plastic face, 1950s, 24" dia., red on white, VG..........$300.00

Light-up counter top "Serve Yourself," 1940 – 50s, EX............$750.00

Light-up fishtail clock, NOS, 1960s, G $240.00

Light-up glass front clock with "Drink Coca-Cola" in red fishtail in center, NOS, in original box, 1960s, M, $550.00.

Neon clock with rainbow panel for 3 to 9 o'clock, "Drink Coca-Cola, Sign of good taste," red and white, 1950s, 36" across, NM, $1,550.00.

Neon clock with spotlighted bottle at 6 o'clock, square, green wrinkle on outer case, 1930s, 16', EX, $825.00.

Photos courtesy Muddy River Trading Co./Gary Metz

Light-up glass front covered clock, white lettering in center on red button, 1950s, NM $600.00

Light-up neon counter, "Pause Drink Coca-Cola," showing bottle spotlighted, restored, rare, and hard-to-find piece, 1930s, EX $4,500.00

Maroon, on wings, 1950s, 17½" dia, EX $250.00

Maroon, on wings with Sprite Boy on each end, it's hard to find these with wings still attached, even harder to find them with the Sprite Boy on the ends, 1950s, 17½" w/o wings, EX $850.00

Metal framed electric with silhouette girl above number 6, 1930 – 40, 18" dia, EX $800.00

Metal framed glass front by Lackner, has bottle in circle above number 6, 1940s, 16" x 16", M $950.00

Neon, octagonal, "Ice Cold Coca-Cola," Silhouette Girl, 1940s, 18", VG $1,600.00

Plastic body electric with fake pendulum and a light-up base with "Coca-Cola" in base, 1970s, G $45.00

Reverse glass metal frame clock "Drink Coca-Cola in bottles" in red center, original jumpstart motor, 1939 – 42, EX, $550.00.

Rocking bottle clock made by Swihart Products, red and green on white background, 1930s, 20", G, $825.00.

Swihart electric Coke clock, unusual size, 1960s, 8" x 6½", EX, $350.00.

Photos courtesy Muddy River Trading Co./Gary Metz

Plastic front electric clock with wave logo on bottom panel, EX..........$40.00

Plastic pocket watch, 1970s, EX..$35.00

Plastic pocket watch shape, "Drink Coca-Cola," 18" dia, EX $45.00

Plastic and metal, "Things go better with Coke," 16" x 16", EX ....$60.00.

Pocket watch, with second hand dial at bottom, VG $75.00

Plastic wood grain effect electric clock, with wave logo at bottom panel, 1970s, EX $15.00

Round, pulsating Silhoutte Girl, cut number 6 on dial, fairly rare, 1930s, 18" dia., EX $2,900.00

Round Silhouette Girl with metal frame, 1930 – 40s, 18" dia, VG..$750.00

Seth Thomas electric "Drink Coca-Cola in Bottles," round, with glass front, 1930s, EX $1,100.00

Telechron, red dot in hour position with white background and white wings, 1948, 36" wing span, VG $450.00

Travel, German made with brass case, 1960s, 3" x 3", EX........$120.00

Bottle stopper and opener, "Glascock Bros. Mfg. Co, Coca-Cola Quality Coolers," 1919 – 20s, EX, $85.00.

Antiques Cards, Collectibles

"Coca-Cola" block print cast iron wishbone, 1900s, EX, $115.00.

"Coca-Cola Bottles" key style, 1930s, EX, $45.00.

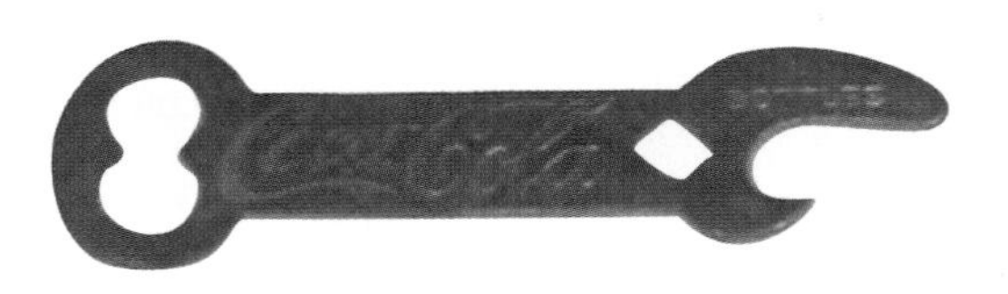

Wall, spring driven pendulum, "Coca-Cola, The Ideal Brain Tonic," Baird Clock Co, 1891 – 95, 24" tall, EX....................................$5,000.00

Wood framed with "Drink Coca-Cola in Bottles" in white on red background, 1930s, 16" x 16", EX $400.00

Wood framed with Silhouette Girl at bottom center, 1930s, 16" x 16", EX $850.00

Wooden case Sessions reproduction clock, hourly chime, 1980, NM $325.00

Openers

Bakelite and metal, 1950s, black, EX $55.00

Bottle shaped, EX $20.00

Bottle shaped, 1950s, EX $100.00

Card suit, stainless steel set in marked carrier sleeves, 1970s, EX $45.00

Cast "Drink Coca-Cola," wall mount, 1930s, EX $10.00

Cigar box cutter "Delicious & Refreshing," 1905 – 15, EX ..$85.00

"Drink Bottled Coca-Cola" saber shaped opener, 1920s, EX, $200.00.

50th Anniversary, 1950s, EX, $55.00.

"Drink Coca-Cola™," straight, 1910 – 50s, EX, $20.00.

Corkscrew, wall mounted, 1920s, EX $75.00

Corkscrew, wall mounted, 1950s, EX $35.00

Cigar box cutter "Delicious & Refreshing," 1905 – 15, EX $85.00

"Drink Coca-Cola in Bottles," 1920 – 40s, EX $20.00

"Drink Coca-Cola in Bottles," brass key, 1910s, EX $100.00

"Drink Coca-Cola™ in Sterilized Bottles," lollipop shaped, 1930s, EX..$85.00

"Drink Coca-Cola," key shaped with bottle cap facsimile at top, 1920 – 50s, EX $35.00

"Drink Coca-Cola," plastic and metal, red and white, EX $3.00

Fishtail spinner, 1910–30, EX..$150.00

Flat metal, 1950s, EX $35.00

"Have a Coke," beer type, G ..$5.00

Nashville, Tenn., celebrating 50th Anniversary, metal, gold plated bottle shaped with opener at bottom of bottle, 1952, EX $75.00

Starr "X" wall mount in original box, 1940 – 80, EX, $5.00.

"The Coca-Cola Bottling Co.," blade has to be marked Kaster & Co. Coca-Cola Bottling Co., Germany, 1905 – 15, brass. Beware: Reproductions exist. EX, $400.00.

Opener, formed hand version, several versions exist, 1930s, G......$25.00

Opener and spoon combination, 1930s, EX $125.00

75th Anniversary from Columbus, Ohio, plastic and metal, 1970s, EX.......................................$15.00

Turtle style with four devices, "Drink Coca-Cola in Bottles," 1970s, EX $12.00

Wall mounted metal "Drink Coca-Cola," also has been referred to as bent metal opener, 1950, EX ..$20.00

Knives

Bone handle combination knife and opener, red lettering, "Drink Coca-Cola in Bottles," 1915 – 25, EX $125.00

Bone handle, two blade, "Delicious and Refreshing," 1920, VG..$100.00

"The Coca-Cola Bottling Co.," blade has to be marked Kaster & Co. Coca-Cola Bottling Co., Germany, 1905 – 15, brass. Beware: Reproductions exist. EX................$400.00

"The Coca-Cola™ Bottling Co.," embossed on side, 1940s, EX..$45.00

One blade and one opener, "Coca-Cola Bottling Company," 1910s, EX, $225.00.

Pearl handle with corkscrew blade and opener, 1930s, EX, $110.00.

Two blade, "Drink Coca-Cola," G, $35.00.

Combination Henry Sears & Son, Solingen, one blade with case shaped like boot as opener, "Coca-Cola," 1920s, white, EX $400.00

"Compliments – The Coca-Cola™ Co.," 1930s, EX $75.00

"Drink Coca-Cola™ in Bottles," 1940, EX $75.00

One blade and one opener, "Coca-Cola Bottling Company," 1910s, EX..$225.00

Small metal utility with cutting blade, opener, and nail file with key chain, "Enjoy Coca-Cola," EX $12.00

Stainless steel with one blade and nail file, 1950 – 60s, EX $30.00

Switchblade, Remington, "Drink Coca-Cola in Bottles," 1930s, EX $225.00

Truck shaped from seminar, 1972, EX $12.00

Two blade pen knife, "Enjoy Coca-Cola," all metal, EX................$15.00

"When Thirsty Try A Bottle" embossed on side with bottle, 1910, EX $350.00

Bulb type handle, large, 1920s, VG, $60.00.

Ice pick and bottle opener, 1920s, VG, $45.00.

Muddy River Trading Co./Gary Metz

Ashtray with bottle lighter featuring "Drink" logo from Canadian bottler red & white, 1950s, NM, $250.00.

Ice Picks

Squared wooden handle advertising "Coca-Cola in Bottles" and "Ice-Coal Phone 87," 1930 – 40s, EX $25.00

Wooden handle, bottle opener in the handle end, 1930, EX $40.00

Wooden handle, 1960s, EX ..$10.00

Ashtrays

Bronze colored, depicting 50th Anniversary in center, 1950s, EX.............$55.00

"Drink Coca-Cola™," round, 1960, EX $5.00

"Drink Coca-Cola™," round with scalloped edge, 1950s, EX $8.00

Glass from Dickson, Tenn., EX..$15.00

"High in energy, Low in calories," tin, 1950s, EX $20.00

Metal with molded cigarette holder, EX $20.00

"The pause that refreshes & J.J. Flynn Co.," square glass, red round center, 1950s, EX $65.00

Top match pull, Bakelite, rare, 1940s, EX, $700.00.

Bakelite lighter and pen holder, 1950s, EX, $130.00.

Set of four, ruby red, price should be doubled if set is in original box, 1950s, EX $350.00

"Support Your Fireman, Compliments of Coca-Cola," tin rectangular, EX $225.00

Wave logo from Mexico, 1970s, EX $3.00

Lighters

Dispose-a-lite in original box, 1970s, EX $15.00

"Drink Coca-Cola," 1950s, EX..$30.00

"Enjoy Coca-Cola" on bottom, flip top, gold plate, NM................$85.00

Executive award, 1984, NM ..$30.00

Musical, red "Drink" on white dot, EX $155.00

Red lettering on the diagonal, goldtone background, 1962, EX $135.00

Round with diamond shaped pattern, "Enjoy Coca-Cola," 1960s, EX ..$35.00

Silver with embossed bottle, flip top, M $35.00

Holder, tin, "Drink Coca-Cola in Bottles," 1940s, F, $350.00.

Matchbook holder with matches, metal, 1959, EX, $110.00.

Muddy River Trading Co./Gary Metz

Porcelain match striker, "Drink Coca-Cola, Strike matches here," 1939, NM, $400.00.

Matches

Book, 50th Anniversary, 1936, EX $8.00

Book, "A Distinctive Drink in a Distinctive Bottle," 1922, EX $100.00

Book from the Coca-Cola Bottling Co. at Fulton, Ky., Telephone 447, EX $2.00

Book, "Have a Coke," bottle in hand, 1940–50s, VG $5.00

Book, "Have a Coke," 1950s, VG ..$5.00

Book for Westinghouse coolers for the Bottlers of Coca-Cola, G ..$2.00

Matchbook holder, celluloid, 1910, EX $300.00

Matchbook holder, "Compliments of The Coca-Cola Co., Coca-Cola Relieves Fatigue," 1907, EX....$300.00

Matchbook holder, "Drink Coca-Cola at Soda Fountains 5¢," 1907, EX $350.00

Safe, "Drink Coca-Cola in Bottles," 1908, NM $600.00

Paper program for the 37th National Convention in Miami, Fla. Oct. 10, 11, 12, 13 (55), American Legion, Drink Coca-Cola, 1955, VG, $30.00.

Bottle bag, used in the days of "wet" coolers to keep the customer dry, 1931, EX, $5.00.

Bottle bag, the distinctive Coca-Cola glass, EX, $5.00.

Coasters

Cardboard, "Go with Coke," 1960s, red and white, EX....................$5.00

"Drink Coca-Cola ice cold," with Silhouette Girl, 1940s, M $12.00

Foil showing hand in bottle with globe behind, square, M $5.00

Foil showing lady with a bottle, square, M..................................$5.00

Foil showing party tray and cooler, square, M.................................$5.00

Foil showing street car scene, M ..$5.00

"Have a Coke" with Sprite Boy, 1940s, M $8.00

Metal with Juanita, 1984, EX $5.00

Metal with Santa Claus, white, EX..$5.00

No Drip Protectors

Bottle protector, 1934, EX $4.00

Bottle protector, 1944, EX $3.00

Bottle protector, 1948, EX $3.00

Bottle protector, 1932, VG, $5.00.

Muddy River Trading Co./Gary Metz

Cardboard menu board, "Sign of Good Taste," with bottle on each side of board, difficult to locate in cardboard, 1959, 19" x 28" NM, $180.00.

Cardboard and wood in tin frame menu board for pricing 6.5 and 12 oz. Coke, this piece isn't found very often, red on black, 1950s, 25" x 15", G, $145.00.

Muddy River Trading Co./Gary Metz

Featuring a couple dancing, 1946, NM $3.00

"A Great Drink...With Good Things To Eat," 1938, NM $3.00

"In Bottles" bottle protector, 1930, NM $3.00

Paper bottle protector, 1946, EX..$3.00

"The Pause That Refreshes," featuring three bottles, 1936, NM $3.00

Rear view of man drinking from a bottle, 1936, NM......................$3.00

Menu Boards

"Drink Coca-Cola Specials Today," 1930s, G..............................$175.00

Kay Displays, "Drink" on spotlight with full glass, gold tone slots on both sides, 1940 – 50s, 36" x 12", EX....................$475.00

Kay Displays, wood with metal trim, "Drink Coca-Cola," 1940s, EX $450.00

Kay Displays, wood and metal with button at center, 1930s, EX....$275.00

Metal Canadian, "Drink Coca-Cola Specials to-day," embossed, scarce and difficult to locate, 1938, 17" x 24", NM, $650.00.

Metal French Canadian board, embossed, 1938, 17" x 24", F, $45.00.

Plywood Kay Displays menu board with "Drink" logo at top, 1930 – 40s, 20" x 37", G, $325.00.

Photos courtesy Muddy River Trading Co./Gary Metz

Kay Displays, 1940 – 50s, 3" x 1" NM $2,400.00

Light-up design with clock, 1960s, EX $125.00

Metal menu board "Drink Coca-Cola, Specials today," 1939, 19" x 27", NM $875.00

Metal and wood, "Drink Coca-Cola" in white lettering inside red fishtail on green background, metal menu strips, 1950s, VG..............................$125.00

Tin, arched top embossed with fishtail design at top, NM..........$375.00

Tin, die cut, "Drink Coca-Cola Be Refreshed," Canadian, 1950, EX..$210.00

Tin, "Drink Coca-Cola" at top edge with "Specials Today" printed above blackboard section on bottom, 1934, 20" x 28", VG........................$350.00

Tin menu board with "Drink" at top in red and featuring silhouette girl in lower right, 1940s, 20" x 28", EX $300.00

Tin, "Specials Today, Coca-Cola" oval at top and bottle in lower right hand side, blackboard for easy menu changes, 1929, 20" x 28", F..$150.00

Wood and masonite Kay Displays menu board featuring a 16" button at top center, manufactured to resemble leather, 17" x 29", EX, $525.00.

Wood and metal Kay Displays menu board, rare and hard to find, 1940s, F, $500.00.

Aluminum door push, bottle shaped with "Drink" in circle overhead, aluminum and red, 1930s, NM, $210.00.

Photos courtesy Muddy River Trading Co./Gary Metz

Wave logo at top, 1970s, 20" x 28", M $30.00

Door Pushes

Aluminum bottle, 1930 – 40, NM $275.00

"Drink Coca-Cola/Ice Cold/In Bottles," porcelain, red and white lettering on red and white background, 35" long, NM.......................$255.00

Metal and plastic, "Drink Coca-Cola Delicious Refreshing," 1930 – 40s, EX $110.00

Metal and plastic, "Have a Coke!" on door attachment, 1930, NM $135.00

Porcelain "Buvez Coca-Cola Glace" door push, red & white on red & yellow, 1950s, 32" long, NM $100.00

Porcelain "Buvez Coca-Cola Glace," French Canadian, yellow & white on red, 32" long, NM $130.00

Porcelain, "Come In! Have a Coca-Cola," yellow and white lettering on red background, 3½" x 11½", NM $290.00

Porcelain "Coke is it" with two wave logo boxes, white on red, 1970s, NM, $65.00.

Porcelain "Ice Cold Coca-Cola In Bottles," 1930s, 30" x 2½", NM, $300.00.

Porcelain, "Ice Cold Coca-Cola In Bottles" on front with "Thank You, Call Again" on reverse side, white lettering on red background, 1930s, 25" x 3¼", NM, $475.00.

Porcelain "Take some Coca-Cola Home Today," white lettering on red, 1950s, 34" long, NM, $525.00.

Photos courtesy Muddy River Trading Co./Gary Metz

Porcelain, French Canadian horizontal push, yellow, white lettering on red, 6½" x 3¼", NM $120.00

Porcelain, French push with wave logo in red & white box at left, white on black with red & white logo, 1970s – 80s, NM $30.00

Porcelain "Ice Cold Coca-Cola In Bottles," red & white on white & red, 1950's, 30" long, NM $550.00

Porcelain "Ice Cold Coca-Cola In Bottles," white lettering on red background, 1950s, 35" long, EX $200.00

Porcelain, "Ice Cold in Bottles," red on white, 1960s, 30", EX......$250.00

Porcelain "Iced Coca-Cola Here," Canadian, white & yellow on red, 1950s, 32" long, NM $225.00

Porcelain, "Pull" at top of plate, "Refresh Yourself Drink Coca-Cola," green, white, and red, 1950s, 4" x 8", EX $450.00

Porcelain, "Refresh Yourself, Drink Coca-Cola," "Push" at top of plate, green, white, and red, 1950s, 4" x 8", NM $525.00

Steel with heavy paint featuring wave logo, white on black with red & white logo, 1970 – 80s, NM, $55.00.

Tin push plate with Silhouette Girl in yellow spotlight, "Drink Coca-Cola delicious refreshing," red with white & yellow lettering, 1939, 28" x 3½", NM, $500.00.

Porcelain, "Thanks Call Again for a Coke," very heavy piece, Canadian, yellow and white on red, 3½" x 13½", NM, $300.00.

Photos courtesy Muddy River Trading Co./Gary Metz

Porcelain and wrought iron, adjustable, "Drink Coca-Cola" in center, 1930s, EX $260.00

Porcelain and wrought iron, "Drink Coca-Cola," 1930s, EX $425.00

Porcelain, "Thanks Call again for a Coca-Cola," yellow and white lettering on red, Canadian, 1930s, EX $200.00

Tin, "Refresh Yourself," 1940 – 50, 3" x 6", G $250.00

Tin, "Refresh Yourself," 1940 – 50, 3" x 6", NM $330.00

Tin, silhouette, 1939 – 41, 33" x 3½", EX.............................$375.00

Trucks

Barclay open bed, even load, 1950, 2", yellow, EX $175.00

Buddy L, "Enjoy Coca-Cola," complete with hand truck that mounts in side compartment, add $15.00 if MIB, 1970, EX $45.00

Buddy L #420C, 1978, G $20.00

Buddy L #4969, scarce tractor-trailer rig, 1970s, NM $80.00

Buddy L with cases and bottles, 1960s, EX, $250.00.

"Big Wheel," "Drink Coca-Cola," add $30.00 if MIB, 1970, EX, $50.00.

Muddy River Trading Co./Gary Metz

Maxitoys made in Holland, hard to find since only 500 were made, 1980s, 11" long, NM, $300.00.

Buddy L #4973 set, 7 pieces, 1970s, NM $55.00

Buddy L #5216 plastic A-frame, will hold eight cases, in original box, 1962, yellow, EX $375.00

Buddy L #5426, pressed steel, 1960, 15", NMIB............................$500.00

Buddy L #5426 truck, steel, Ford style with chrome grille, 1960s, yellow, NM................................$110.00

Chevy delivery, tin, Smokeyfest Estb. 1930, 1995, MIB $25.00

Corgi Jr. featuring contour logo, 1982, NM $18.00

El Camino given away at convention in Ohio, plastic, 1995, red and white, MIB $15.00

Marx #991, pressed steel, Sprite Boy decal, 1950s, gray, MIB $1,000.00

Marx #1090, tin, open bed, 1956, 17", yellow and red, EX $450.00

Marx, if in MIB condition with original box this value would nearly double, 1950, G $225.00

Muddy River Trading Co./Gary Metz

Plastic Marx Canadian truck with 6 plastic cases, wooden wheels, in original box, hard to find, red, 1950s, 11", G, $1,300.00.

Muddy River Trading Co./Gary Metz

Sanyo truck made in Japan, distributed by Allen Haddock Company in Atlanta, Ga., with original box, battery operated, 1960s, 12½" long, EX, $275.00.

Vending machine style 1/25 scale model kit, 1970, MIB, $75.00.

Matchbox with even load bed, "Drink Coca-Cola," 1960s, 2", yellow, EX $65.00

Metalcraft #171 A-frame, 1932, red and yellow, EX $900.00

Model T, scale kit in original box, 1970s, MIB $55.00

Smith-Miller A-frame, wood and aluminum, rubber tires, 1944, 14", red, EX $1,600.00

Supervan, plastic, 1970s, 18"x11", NM $110.00

Tin van, "Drink Coca-Cola, Delicious, Refreshing," Japanese, 1950, 4", yellow $150.00

"Big Wheel," "Drink Coca-Cola," add $30.00 if MIB, 1970, EX....$50.00

Marx, if in MIB condition with original box this value would nearly double, 1950, G $225.00

Van, cardboard, Max Headroom, 1980s, 6", NM $10.00

VW van with friction motor by Taiyo, 1950s, 7½" long, VG ..$225.00

Muddy River Trading Co./Gary Metz

Buddy Lee composition doll with original uniform bearing the original Lee tag, 1950s, 12" tall, EX, $875.00.

Dispenser with original glasses, "Drink Coca-Cola," 1950s, EX, $100.00.

Bang gun, "It's the real thing," M, $20.00.

Toys

American Flyer kite, bottle at tail end of kite, 1930s, EX..........$400.00

American Flyer train car, "Pure As Sunlight," a complete train set with track and original box would push this price to around $4,000.00, 1930s, red and green, EX $1,200.00

Bean bag, "Enjoy Coca-Cola," with dynamic wave, 1970s, red, VG..$20.00

Bicycle, EX $300.00

Boomerang, 1950s, EX..........$25.00

Bus, cardboard double decker with dynamic contour logo, Sweetcentre, 1980s, red, M..........................$35.00

Caboose with wave logo, 1970s, 6½" long, EX.................................$45.00

Coca-Cola train set, still in original box, 1974, M $350.00

Corvette, die cast, convention banquet gift, 1993, MRFB $20.00

"Express Cafe Snackbar," plastic and tin, "Drink Coca-Cola" button on front and advertisement on back, 1950 – 60s, NM...................$150.00

Muddy River Trading Co./Gary Metz

Roller skates, embossed "Drink Coca-Cola in Bottles" on the face with "Pat. Aug. 16, 1914" under first line, probably from the St. Louis Bottling Company, 1914, VG, $900.00.

Shopping basket, child's size with grocery graphics printed on both sides of basket liner, complete with contents, 1950s, EX, $400.00.

Jump rope with whistle in one handle, "Pure as Sunlight" on other handle, 1920s, G $350.00

Metal can bank commemerating 75th anniversary, red and white, 12 oz. can, riverside, G $15.00

Model airplane with Coca-Cola circle for wings, 1960s, red and white, EX $40.00

Pedal car, white lettering, 1940–1950, 19" x 36", red, EX $1,300.00

Stove, "Drink Coca-Cola with Your Meals," 1930s, green, EX..$2,000.00

Top, spinning, plastic 2-color, Memphis, Tenn., bottler, red & white, 1½" x 1½", Riverside, EX $10.00

Whistle, plastic, "Merry Christmas Coca-Cola Bottling, Memphis Tenn.," 1950, EX...................$10.00

Whistle, wood, "Drink Coca-Cola," 1940s, EX $30.00

Games

Baseball bat, 1950s, EX $175.00

Baseball bat, wooden, featuring Coca-Cola at end, 1968, EX ..$50.00

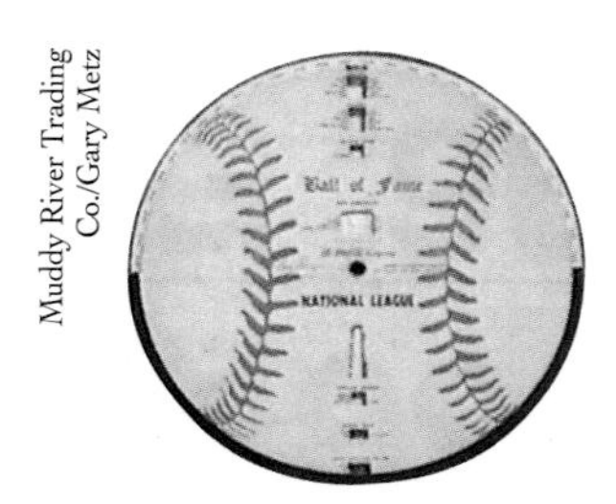

Muddy River Trading Co./Gary Metz

Baseball Hall of Fame information featuring both National and American League from 1901 to 1960, baseball shaped, 1960, G, $80.00.

Baseball glove, left handed, MacGregor, 1970, EX, $175.00.

Muddy River Trading Co./Gary Metz

Game box, contains two decks of 1943 cards unopened, plus marbles, dominos, chess, and checkers, 1940s, NM, $450.00.

Baseball glove, left handed, 1920s, EX $350.00

Bingo card with slide covers, "Play Refreshed Drink Coca-Cola From Sterilized Bottles," 1930s, EX..$45.00

Broadsides, Milton Bradley, 1940 – 50s, G...................................$100.00

Checkers, modern, 1970s, EX..$50.00

Checkers, wooden, Coca-Cola name in script on top, 1940 – 50s, EX $45.00

Chinese Checkers board with Silhouette Girl logo, 1930 – 40s, EX..$75.00

Dominos, wooden in original box, 1940 – 50s, EX $55.00

Football, miniature, 1960s, black and white, EX $10.00

Game set, contains checkers dominos, cribbage, plus two unopened deck of 1943 cards, 1940s, 10½" x 11½", NM $400.00

Gold box, 1974, M $15.00

Playing cards, Atlanta Christmas, 1992, EX....................................$45.00

Playing cards, EX $85.00

Muddy River Trading Co./Gary Metz

Playing cards, complete with Joker and Bridge scoring cards, featuring girl with bottle, 1928, NM, $2,500.00.

Playing cards, double deck in container similar to six pack holder, 1970s, EX, $50.00.

Playing cards, from Campbellsville, Ky., Bottling Co., M, $65.00.

Playing cards, Betty, 1977, M ..$30.00

Playing cards, Blue wheat, 1938, M..$135.00

Playing cards, Bottle and food, 1974, M $25.00

Playing cards, "Coca-Cola adds life to everything nice," 1976, M ..$40.00

Playing cards, Coca-Cola and Don Nelson of the Milwaukee Bucks, 1970s, M $55.00

Playing cards, "Coke Is It," 1985, M $25.00

Playing cards, Couple at beach with surf board, 1963, M $95.00

Playing cards, Cowgirl in hat with a bottle, 1951, M $80.00

Playing cards, "Drink Coca-Cola in Bottles," 1938, green wheat, EX $150.00

Playing cards, "Drink Coca-Cola in Bottles," 1938, red wheat, M..$135.00

Playing cards, Dynamic wave trademark, 1985, M........................$20.00

Playing cards from the California Chapter of the Cola Clan, 1986, EX ..$100.00

Playing cards, lady with dog and bottle, 1943, EX, $175.00.

Playing cards, model that was used on 1923 calendar, 1977, M, $45.00.

Playing cards, friends and family, 1980, M, $55.00.

Playing cards, Girl at beach, 1956, M....................................... $75.00

Playing cards, Girl in pool, "Sign of Good Taste," 1959, EX..........$75.00

Playing cards, Girl putting on ice skates, 1956, M $75.00

Playing cards, Girl sitting in field, 1974, M $25.00

Playing cards, Great Bend, Kansas, EX $175.00

Playing cards, "Have a Coke and a Smile," double deck, 1979, EX..$35.00

Playing cards, Horse Race, in original box, EX $300.00

Playing cards, Kansas City Spring Fling '82, M $55.00

Playing cards, Lady at party with a bottle, 1951, M $80.00

Playing cards, Louisville, Ky., convention, 1980s, NRFB $12.00

Playing cards, Military nurse in uniform, 1943, EX $135.00

Playing cards, "Refresh," 1958, M $75.00

Playing cards, "Refreshing New Feeling," featuring couple in front of fireplace, 1963, M, $65.00.

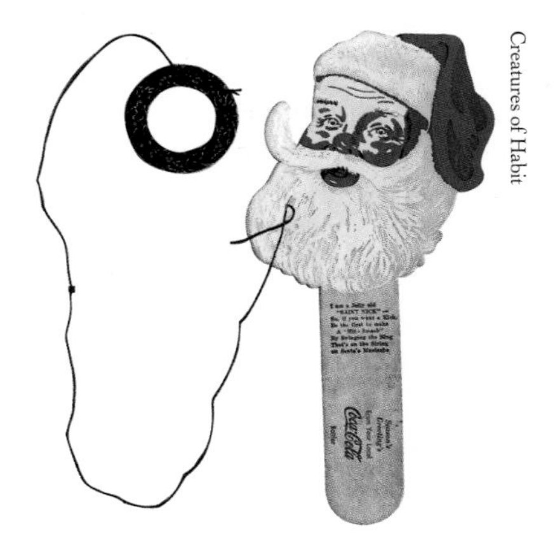

Creatures of Habit

Ring toss game with Santa Claus at top of handle, VG, $15.00.

Sprite Boy Double Six Domino set in original vinyl case, 1970s, EX, $25.00.

Playing cards, Santa Claus, 1979, M $25.00

Playing cards, Smokeyfest Chapter, 1994, EX $25.00

Playing cards, Smokeyfest Chapter, 1995, EX $20.00

Playing cards, Snowman in a bottle cap hat, 1959, M $65.00

Playing cards, Spotter lady, 1943, M....................................$100.00

Playing cards, Sprite Boy and bottle, 1979, M $35.00

Playing cards, Woman in uniform with wings below photo, 1943, EX $125.00

Pool cue, featuring dynamic wave logo, EX $55.00

Jewelry

Belt and buckle, "All Star Dealer Campaign Award," 1950 – 60s, M........$25.00

Brooch, "Drink Coca-Cola," EX ..$35.00

Button, pin lock, bottle is hand club pen, VG $12.00

Muddy River Trading Co./Gary Metz

Coca-Cola 100th anniversary wrist watch, featuring a diamond chip at 12 o'clock, NM, $120.00.

Muddy River Trading Co./Gary Metz

Watch fob with likeness of Duster Girl, Coca-Cola logo on reverse side, 1911, E, $800.00.

Necklace, medallion, with Hilda Clark likeness in center, 1970s, VG, $25.00.

Charm bracelet with bottle and glass charms, EX $125.00

Coca-Cola Bottlers convention pin, shield shaped, 1912, EX $500.00

Coca-Cola Bottling Company annual convention pin, 1915, red, white, blue, EX...............................$600.00

Coca-Cola Bottling Company annual convention pin, 1916, EX......$600.00

Compact with 50th Anniversary spot on center front, 1950s, red, M..$35.00

Cuff links, gold finish, "Enjoy Coca-Cola," glass shaped, 1970s, EX $30.00

Hat pin from driver's uniform, "Drink Coca-Cola," 1930, EX.............$175.00

Money clip, compliments Coca-Cola Bottling Works, Nashville, Tenn., EX $45.00

Necklace with bottle, EX $75.00

Service pin, 15 year, EX $75.00

Snap lid with raised bottle in center, all metal, EX $75.00

Bandanna, Kit Carson, new, white, EX, $15.00.

Bandanna, Kit Carson, 1950s, 20" x 22", red, EX, $65.00.

Driver's folding cap, 1950s, $65.00.

Clothing

Belt, vinyl, with "Drink Coca-Cola" blocks, 1960, white, VG $15.00

Bow tie, white "Coca-Cola" on red, NM $35.00

Bowler's shirt, "Things go better with Coke," 1960s, EX.......... $20.00

Cap, felt beanie, 1930 – 40s, 8" dia, VG $45.00

Cowboy hat, convention, 1937, EX $200.00

Driver's cap with hard bill, red, white, and yellow, 1930s, EX $75.00

Driver's shirt, short sleeve, white with green stripes and large back patch with white background, VG $35.00

Hat, soda person, cloth, 1940, EX $25.00

Hat, soda person, note the term Soda Jerk wasn't coined until the 1940s, EX $20.00

Hat, soda person, paper fold-up, featuring Sprite Boy, 1950s, VG ..$25.00

Kerchief, "The Cola Clan," with Silhouette Girl from Coca-Cola Collectors' banquet, 1970s, white and red, VG, $12.00.

Patch, "Coca-Cola," red outline and lettering on white background, VG, $8.00.

Patch, small shirt, "Drink Coca-Cola," with red and black lettering, 1960s, EX, $5.00.

Painter's hat, 1950s, F............$10.00

Patch, "Drink Coca-Cola in Bottles" with yellow and white lettering, 1960s, red, EX..........................$8.00

Patch, large, back, "Enjoy Coca-Cola," with yellow and white lettering, 1950 – 60s, red, EX $15.00

Tie, clip-on of Coca-Cola bottle caps, red, yellow, and green on blue, EX $15.00

Tie, Coca-Cola in stars, white lettering on blue field, EX $20.00

Wallets

Coin purse, leather, gold embossed lettering, "Drink Coca-Cola in Bottles, Delicious, Refreshing" with rounded metal snap top that is gold colored, 1910, black, EX $150.00

Coin purse, leather, silver colored rounded metal snap top, silver embossed lettering, 1920s, black, EX $150.00

Coin purse, snap closure top, leather, compliments of Coca-Cola Bottling Co, Memphis, Tenn., 1910 – 20s, VG $185.00

Coin purse with gold lettering engraved in leather, "When thirsty try a bottle," "Coca-Cola Bottling Company" with a paper label bottle to the left of lettering, 1907, maroon, EX, $100.00.

Cardboard cut out, "Free Decorations in cartons of Coke," Santa standing on ladder in front of Christmas tree with a small girl on stool at bottom of ladder, 1960s, $10.00.

Coin purse, snap closures, leather, arrow, "Whenever you see an arrow think of Coca-Cola," 1909, VG ..$175.00

Embossed bottle on front, 1920s, black, EX................................$35.00

Leather, black, 1920s, EX......$80.00

Leather, "Drink Coca-Cola, Delicious, Refreshing," 1920s, EX..$30.00

Leather with gold embossed lettering, 1907, black, EX $90.00

Plastic, "Enjoy Coca-Cola," 1960s, black, EX..................................$8.00

Trifold with calendar, leather with gold embossed lettering, 1918, black, EX...............................$85.00

Trifold with calendar and photo sleeves, leather, gold embossed lettering, 1920s, black, EX $75.00

Santas

Banner, horizontal paper, Santa Claus, "The gift for thirst," 1952, G $40.00

Black Rushton doll holding a bottle, one of the harder dolls to find, 1970s, 16" tall, EX................$225.00

Cardboard cut out sign featuring Sprite Boy and Santa Claus with reindeer, has original easel back attachment, 1940s, 26" x 52", EX, $525.00.

Cardboard Santa hanger, "Add Zest to the Season," Canadian, 1949, 10½" x 18½", EX, $900.00.

Cardboard die cut hanging sign "Christmas Greetings," 1932, NM, $4,200.00.

Photos courtesy Muddy River Trading Co./Gary Metz

Cardboard cut out, "Free new Holiday Ideas in Cartons of Coke," Santa standing on ladder with small child playing with a jack-in-the-box on floor, 1960s, 36", EX $20.00

Cardboard cut out of Santa in front of an open refrigerator door holding a bottle, this folds in the middle, easel back, 1948, 5' tall, F....$225.00

Cardboard cut out, Santa Claus, "The gift for thirst," 1953, 9" x 18", EX......................................$200.00

Cardboard cut out, Santa Claus, "Greetings," ribbon on bottom, G $350.00

Cardboard cut out showing small boy peering around a door, facing Santa who's opening a bottle, easel back, 3-dimensional, 1950s, VG $175.00

Cardboard cut out, "Things go better with Coke," Santa and little boy with dog, 1960s, 36", EX $20.00

Cardboard stand up Santa Claus holding three bottles in each hand with a button behind Santa, 1950s, VG $175.00

Cardboard stand up Santa Claus resting one arm on a post, holding a bottle with the other, holly Christmas wreath is shown in rear, 1960s, EX $75.00

Muddy River Trading Co./Gary Metz

Cardboard truck sign featuring Santa with both hands full of Coke bottles "Santa's Helpers," 1960's, 66" x 32", G, $120.00.

Poster, cardboard, cut out, "Season's Greetings," Santa sitting in the middle of a train set with a white helicopter flying around his head, 1962, 32"x47", EX, $325.00.

Light hanger, 1960, EX, $12.00.

Carton stuffer Santa Claus, "Good taste for all," EX $45.00

Christmas card, management and employees of Ruston Coca-Cola Bottling Company, four color, 14" x 5½", EX $4.00

Christmas card with possible origin of Santa clothing on reverse side, G..$35.00

Cut out Santa Claus on stool holding wooden rabbit, EX $85.00

Display topper, cardboard, "Stock up for the Holidays," Santa holding a bottle behind a six pack, 1950s, EX $125.00

Paper hanger, Seasons Greetings with Santa and helicopter, 1962, 16" x 24", NM $425.00

Porcelain, large animated Santa with a bottle, holding up a finger to quiet a small porcelain dog, new, EX..$110.00

Poster, cardboard, vertical, "The gift for thirst, Stock up for the Holidays," children with presents and a hatless Santa with a bottle, EX.............$40.00

Royal Orleans LE plate, 1983, NM $50.00

Royal Orleans LE plate, 1983, F..$15.00

Santa doll in black boots, original, 1950s, 16", EX, $175.00.

Muddy River Trading Co./Gary Metz

Sign, cardboard rocket, "Drink Coca-Cola Festive Holidays," die cut dimensional Santa, 1950s, 33" tall, VG, $260.00.

Axe, "For Sportsmen" "Drink Coca-Cola," 1930, EX, $800.00.

Royal Orleans LE plate in original box, 1983, NM $80.00

Royal Orleans Santa plate, first plate, 1983, MIB $75.00

Sign, cardboard, double sided hanging, "Things go better with Coke," Santa and a couple kissing, 1960, 13½" x 16", EX $45.00

Sign, cardboard, "Santa's Helpers," Santa holding six bottles, 1950s, VG $75.00

Wreath, cardboard, Santa holding six bottles, 1958, EX.............$20.00

Miscellaneous

Astro-Float mounts on top of bottle, designed to put ice cream in for a Coke float or ice to help cool down your drink, 1960s, VG....................................$15.00

Badge holder, Bottler's Conference, metal and celluloid, 1943, EX $45.00

Bank, cooler style, "Have a Coke" embossed in top, 1940s, 5" x 5" x 3½", EX $1,000.00

Bookmark, celluloid, "Drink Coca-Cola at Soda Fountains 5¢," 1898, F, $550.00.

Bookmark, plastic with wave logo, 1970, white and red, EX, $5.00.

Muddy River Trading Co./Gary Metz

Bottle lamp, with cap and original marked brass base, very rare and highly desirable, 1920s, 20", NM, $7,200.00.

Bell stamped metal, "Refresh Yourself Drink Coca-Cola In Bottles" on both sides, 1930s, 3¼" tall, NM......$500.00

Bicycle, standard adult size with original packing, NOS, NM $425.00

Bolo tie, Kit Carson, neckerchief in original mailer envelope, 1950s, EX...$75.00

Bookends, bottle shaped, heavy brass, 1963, 8" tall, NM $325.00

Bookmark, celluloid oval, "What Shall We Drink? Drink Coca-Cola 5¢," 1906, 2" x 2¼", EX $700.00

Bookmark, Lillian Nordica, 1904, 2" x 6", EX $230.00

Bookmark, paper, "Drink Coca-Cola Delicious and Refreshing" featuring Lillian Nordica at stand table with a glass, 1900s, 2¼" x 5¼", NM $1,500.00

Bookmark, white cat, Tell City Coca-Cola Bottling Co., Inc., EX $45.00

Bowl, green, scalloped edge Vernonware, "Drink Coca-Cola Ice Cold," 1930s, green, EX........................$450.00

Cardboard display of Coca-Cola bottling plant in San Diego, note the streamline architecture; this has been designated a historic cultural monument, 14" x 4½" x 6½", EX, $50.00.

Cash register topper, "Please Pay When Served," light-up, 1950s, EX, $950.00.

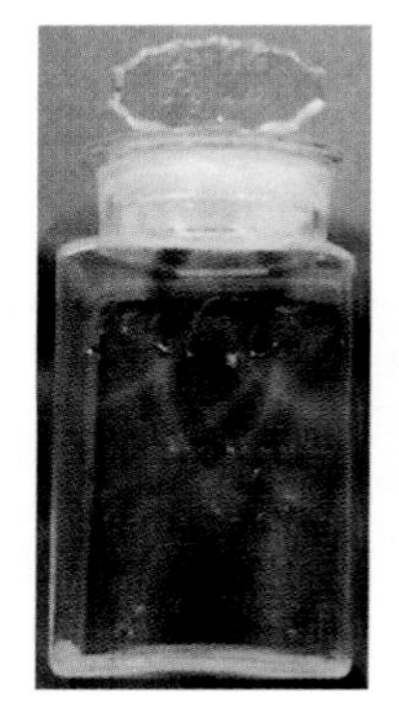

Coke pepsin gum jar with embossed lid, 1905 – 11, NM, $900.00.

Photos courtesy Muddy River Trading Co./Gary Metz

Button, pin-back, featuring "Drink" logo, red lettering on yellow background, ¾" dia., Riverside, G ..$10.00

Card table, bottle in each corner, advertisement sheet under side of table boasts it's so strong it can hold a grownup standing on it, 1930, VG $225.00

Cash register topper, plain version without message, Coca-Cola on top, 11½ x 5", G $475.00

Cash register topper, "Please Pay When Served," wood, glass and chrome, difficult to find, 1940s, 11½" x 6", EX $375.00

Chewing gum display box, held twenty 5¢ packages, cardboard, rare, 1920s, VG $1,500.00

Cigar band, 1930, EX $150.00

Cigarette box, 50th Anniversary frosted glass, 1936, EX $700.00

Coca-Cola Sweetheart box of straws, 1960s, M $75.00

Coke pepsin gum jar, square version with the original lid, hard to find, 05-11, G $775.00

Comb, plastic, 1970s, red, EX....$2.00

Muddy River Trading Co./Gary Metz

Coke pepsin gum jar, with thumb nail type lid, 1903, NM, $475.00.

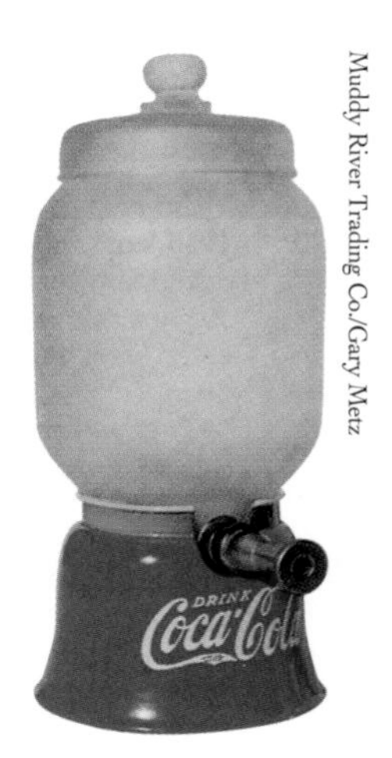

Muddy River Trading Co./Gary Metz

Dispenser with porcelain base, frosted glass body and lid, white lettering on red base, 1920s, 17" tall, NM, $6,200.00.

Creatures of Habit

Educational poster, chart four in the electricity series, distributed to schools for teaching aids, great graphics, but low in demand, 1940s, M, $15.00.

Counter dispenser, bolt on, 1940 – 50s, VG $750.00

Cup, paper, red lettering "Things Go Better With Coke" on white square, 1960s, NM $3.00

Desk pen holder with music box attached, 1950s, EX $250.00

Display bottle, hard rubber, 1948, 4' tall, EX..................................$975.00

Door lock, metal, "Drink Coca-Cola in Bottles, Delicious and Refreshing," 1930s, EX $40.00

Dust cover, Lone Ranger, 1971, EX $35.00

Dust cover, Superman, 1971, EX.....................................$35.00

Fact wheel, United States at a glance, EX $75.00

Fence post topper made from heavy cast iron, used to decorate fence pillars outside bottling plants, has a threaded base, 20" tall, EX $500.00

Flashlight in original box, 1980, EX.......................................$20.00

Muddy River Trading Co./Gary Metz

Globe, milk glass, from ceiling fixture, "Drink Coca-Cola," 1930 – 40s, EX, $450.00.

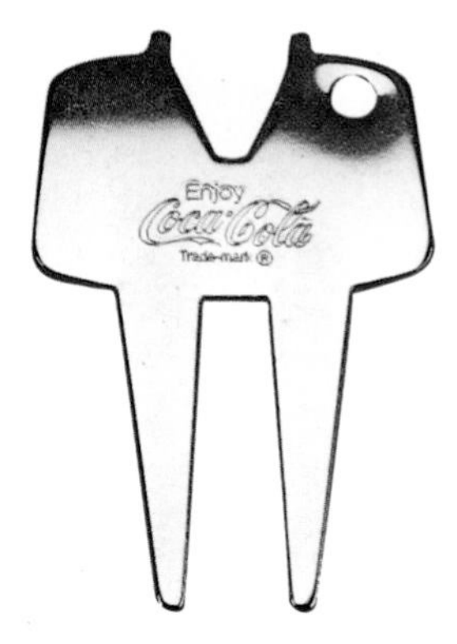

Golf divot remover, metal, EX, $5.00.

Fly swatter, "Drink Coca-Cola In Bottles," EX....................$90.00

45 RPM record, Trini Lopez, with dust cover advertising Fresca, 1967, EX $10.00

Frame for 36" x 20" posters, 1940, 36" x 20" , EX $225.00

Glass negative for the 1940s poster featuring the tennis girl, very unusual and rare, 20" x 24", G $100.00

Globe, leaded glass, round, "Coca-Cola," rare, 1920s, EX......$10,000.00

Globe, milk glass, "Drink Coca-Cola" with trademark incorporated in tail of "C," if with original hardware add $200.00, 1930, EX $650.00

Ice tong with wood handle, "Drink Coca-Cola, Greencastle, Ind.," 1920s, EX $300.00

"Jim Dandy" combination tool that has a screwdriver, button hook, cigar cutter, and bottle opener, rare, 1920, EX $300.00

Jug with paper label in original box, 1960s, one gallon, EX $20.00

Lamp, milk glass, painted, "Coca-Cola" bottle, 1920s, 20" tall, EX, $5,500.00.

Muddy River Trading Co./Gary Metz

Mileage meter, "Travel refreshed," originating from Asheville, N.C., white on red, 1950s, EX, $1,550.00.

Muddy River Trading Co./Gary Metz

Metal string holder with six pack in spotlight, "Take Home In Cartons," red, 1930s, 14" x 16", EX, $1,000.00.

Key tag, Coca-Cola Bottling Co., Indianapolis, showing 2 cents postage guaranteed, VG......$35.00

Light fixture, rectangular colored leaded glass, bottom beaded fringe, "Coca-Cola 5¢," "Pittsburgh Mosaic Glass Co., Inc., Pittsburgh, Pa.," 1910, 11"w x 22" x 7½"h, EX $12,000.00

Light, hanging adjustable, with popcorn insert on one of four sides, with red and white Coca-Cola advertising on the other panels, 1960s, 18" x 18", M $525.00

Magic lantern slide, hand colored glass, "A Home Run" from Advertising Slide Co., St. Louis, 1970s, EX $125.00

Magic lantern slide, hand colored glass, "People say they like it because...," 1920s, EX $100.00

Message pad shaped like a case of Coke, 1980s, EX $8.00

Music box, cooler shaped, in working order, 1950s, EX $130.00

Napkin holder with Sprite Boy panel on side, "Have a Coke 5¢," 1950, VG $700.00

Muddy River Trading Co./Gary Metz

Note pad holder for candlestick phone, price includes phone which also has a courtesy coin box, 1920s, EX, $900.00.

Money bag, vinyl zippered, "Enjoy Coca-Cola," 1960s, VG, $8.00.

Muddy River Trading Co./Gary Metz

Plastic mileage meter from Asheboro, N.C., red, 1950s, F, $1,000.00.

NCAA final four commemorative 16 oz. can and pin set, 1994, EX ..$15.00

Night light, "It's the real thing" with the dynamic wave logo rectangular shaped, 1970s, EX..................$25.00

Paperweight, clear glass bottle cap shaped with "Enjoy Coca-Cola" etched in glass, M $55.00

Pen, baseball bat shaped, 1940s, white and black, EX $50.00

Pen and pencil set by Cross, logo on pocket clips, in original case, M $55.00

Pen and pencil set in plastic case celebrating the 50th anniversary of Coca-Cola Bottling, Frankfort, Ind., 1965, EX $35.00

Pen, ink, red and white, 1950s, EX.......................................$40.00

Pencil box, pencil-shaped, Sprite Boy, 1948, NM $145.00

Pencil holder, celluloid, 1910, EX $135.00

Pencil holder, white with red button, 1950s, 5" tall, NM......................$300.00

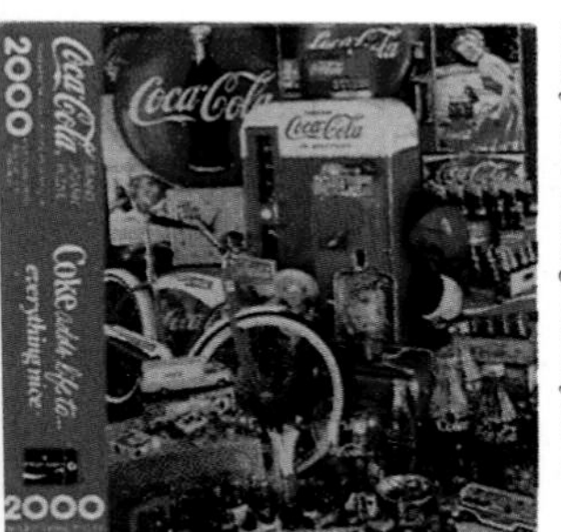

Muddy River Trading Co./Gary Metz

Puzzle, 2,000 piece with box, NM, $25.00.

Refrigerator water bottle, green glass, "Compliments Coca-Cola Bottling Co.," embossed, EX, $125.00.

Muddy River Trading Co./Gary Metz

Ricky Nelson set, consisting of poster and a 45LP, personally autographed, framed, difficult to find these, 1960s, 18" x 14½", G, $575.00.

Pencil, mechanical, 1930s, EX ..$25.00

Penlight, push button with wave logo, 1970s, white and red, EX $8.00

Pepsin gum jar with thumbnail type lid, 1910, EX $450.00

Pocket protector, vinyl, Union City, Tenn., 1950s, red and black, G$15.00

Polaroid camera, "Coke adds life to Happy Times," EX $75.00

Popcorn bucket, "Drink Coca-Cola in Bottles" spot in center, waxed cardboard, 1950s, M................$8.00

Postage stamp carrier, celluloid, 1902, EX $500.00

Pot holder, "Drink Coca-Cola every bottle sterilized," red lettering on yellow, 1910 – 12, G $275.00

Printers block with Sprite Boy, 1940s, M $25.00

Ruler, 12", wooden, "A Good Rule," very common item, 1920 – 60, EX..........$2.00

Sandwich toaster, "Coke," used at soda fountains to toast sandwiches and would imprint the bread, hard to find, 1930s, EX $700.00

Muddy River Trading Co./Gary Metz

Syrup dispenser, reproduction made of hard rubber, 1950s, EX, $325.00.

Shade, colored leaded glass, with the chain edge that originally had a border of hanging beaded fringe, "Property of the Coca-Cola Co. to be returned on demand" must be on top band, 1920s, 18" dia., EX, $4,000.00.

Street marker, brass "Drink Coca-Cola Safety First," fairly rare piece, 1920 VG, $175.00.

School set, "Drink Coca-Cola Delicious Refreshing," complete with pencils, rulers, erasers in box, 1930s, red, EX $65.00

Sewing needles in Coke packaging, featuring the girl at party with the fox fur, 1920s, EX $75.00

Shotgun, model 1500XLT, Coca-Cola Centennial, embossed Coca-Cola on receiver and barrel never fired, 1986, MIB................$1,100.00

Statue holding bottles of Coca-Cola, "Tell me your profit story, please" on base, 1930 – 40s, EX...........$100.00

String dispenser, tin, red with carton in yellow circle, 12" x 16", EX..................................$425.00

Tap knob, doubled sided, "Coke," 1960 – 70, NM $20.00

Tap knob, enameled double sided, "Drink Coke or Coca-Cola, Ask for it Either Way," 1940 – 50s, EX.....................................$70.00

Tape for reel to reel for radio play, contains 16 advertising spots prepared by McCann & Erickson, Inc., New York, New York, 1970s.......................$25.00

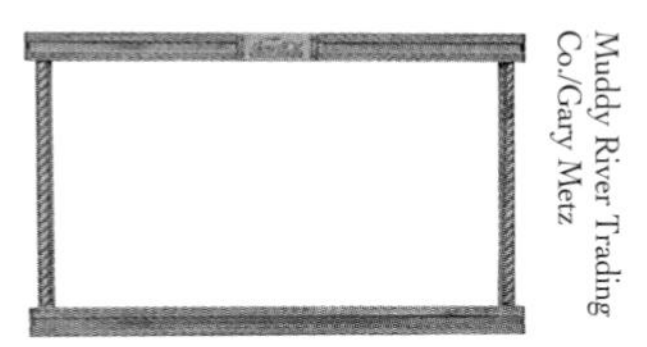

Muddy River Trading Co./Gary Metz

Wooden Kay Displays frame with unusual crest at top, will accommodate 40" x 24" poster, 1930s, F, $160.00.

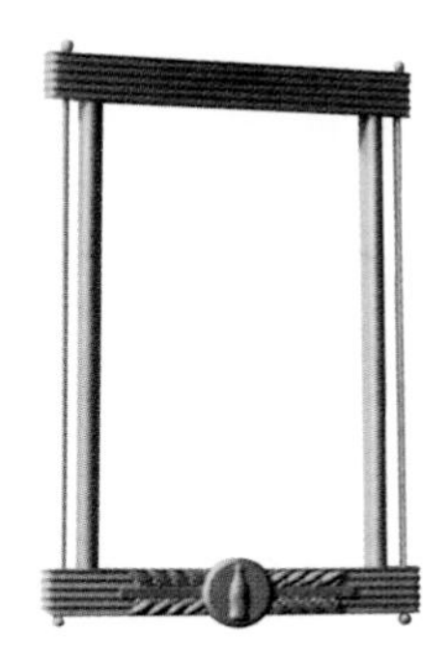

Wooden original Coke frame with crest, gold, 1940s, EX, $300.00.

Wooden transistor radio with battery compartment behind back door, Philippines, 1940s, 7"w x 4"d x 5"t, EX, $375.00.

Photos courtesy Muddy River Trading Co./Gary Metz

Tape measure, horseshoe shaped, Coke advertising on side, NM ..$5.00

Telephone, bottle shaped, new, MIB $15.00

Thimble, "Coca-Cola," red lettering, M $25.00

Tokens, "Free drink Atlanta, Ga.," new, G $1.00

Tokens, "Free Drink 1904 World's Fair," new G $1.00

Tumbler showing "Drink Coca-Cola," 1950 – 70s, EX..............$8.00

Umbrella, orange, black, and white, "Drink Coca-Cola," 1930s, EX $750.00

Wall pocket, 3-dimensional press fiber board, 9" x 13", EX......$450.00

Water cup with handle, tin, "This cup for water but Drink Coca-Cola in Bottles, Coca-Cola Bottling Co. Greencastle, Ind." is printed in black in bottom of cup, rare piece, 1930s, EX $125.00

Winchester model #94, Coca-Cola Centennial, only 2,500 produced, never fired, 1986, MIB $1,200.00

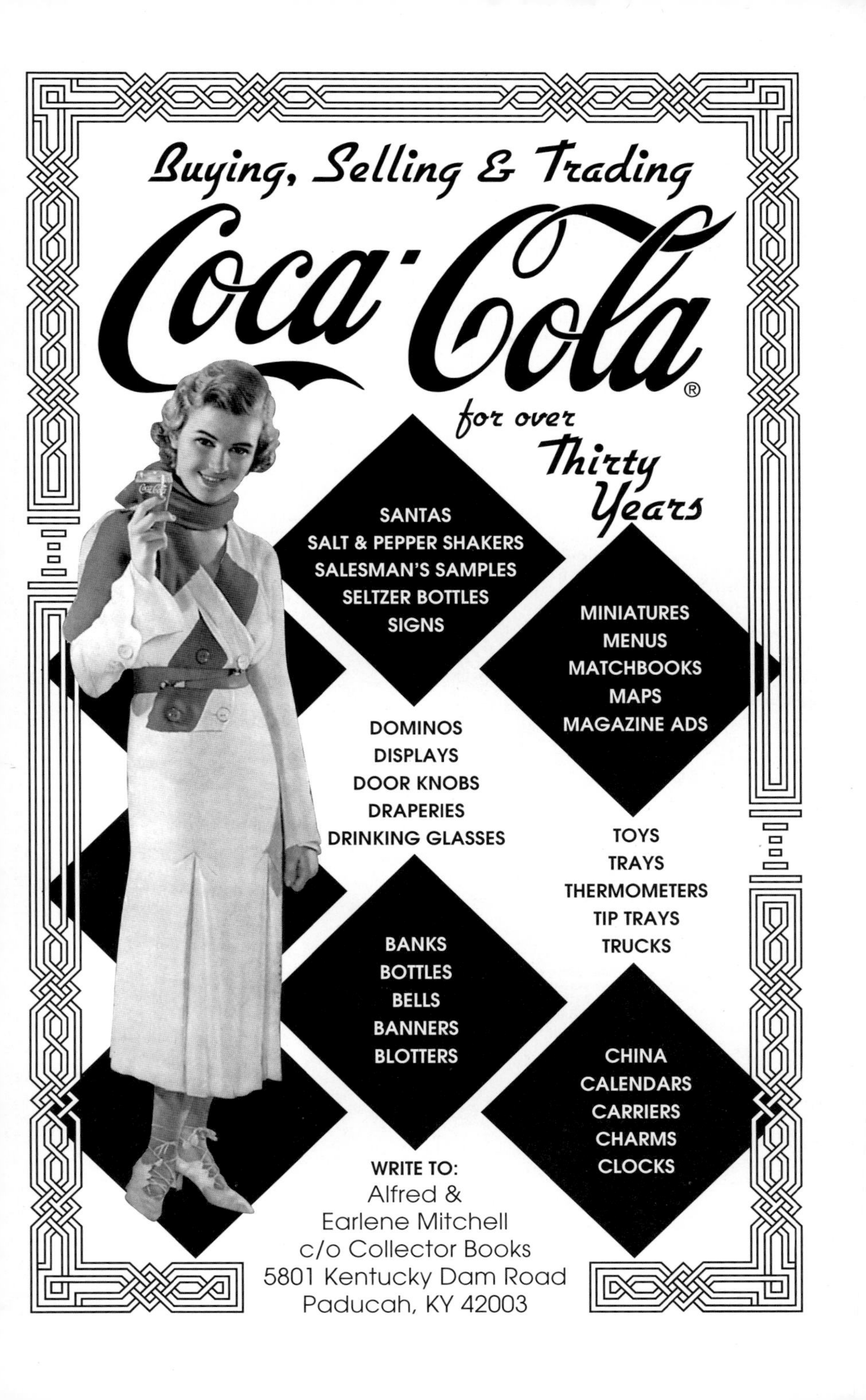

Buying, Selling & Trading
Coca-Cola®
for over Thirty Years
SANTAS
SALT & PEPPER SHAKERS
SALESMAN'S SAMPLES
SELTZER BOTTLES
SIGNS
MINIATURES
MENUS
MATCHBOOKS
MAPS
MAGAZINE ADS
DOMINOS
DISPLAYS
DOOR KNOBS
DRAPERIES
DRINKING GLASSES
TOYS
TRAYS
THERMOMETERS
TIP TRAYS
TRUCKS
BANKS
BOTTLES
BELLS
BANNERS
BLOTTERS
CHINA
CALENDARS
CARRIERS
CHARMS
CLOCKS
WRITE TO:
Alfred &
Earlene Mitchell
c/o Collector Books
5801 Kentucky Dam Road
Paducah, KY 42003